THE DEATH OF SOCRATES

Plato

EDITORIAL DIRECTOR Justin Kestler
EXECUTIVE EDITOR Ben Florman
DIRECTOR OF TECHNOLOGY Tammy Hepps

SERIES EDITORS John Crowther, Justin Kestler
MANAGING EDITOR Vince Janoski

WRITERS Jonathan Weil
EDITORS Matt Blanchard, John Crowther

This edition published by Spark Publishing

Spark Publishing
A Division of SparkNotes LLC
120 Fifth Avenue, 8th Floor
New York, NY 10011

First edition.

Please submit all comments and questions or report errors to www.sparknotes.com/errors

Library of Congress Catalog-in-Publication Data available upon request

Printed and bound in the United States

ISBN 1-58663-820-3

INTRODUCTION:
STOPPING TO BUY SPARKNOTES ON A SNOWY EVENING

Whose words these are you *think* you know.
Your paper's due tomorrow, though;
We're glad to see you stopping here
To get some help before you go.

Lost your course? You'll find it here.
Face tests and essays without fear.
Between the words, good grades at stake:
Get great results throughout the year.

Once school bells caused your heart to quake
As teachers circled each mistake.
Use SparkNotes and no longer weep,
Ace every single test you take.

Yes, books are lovely, dark, and deep,
But only what you grasp you keep,
With hours to go before you sleep,
With hours to go before you sleep.

CONTENTS

CONTEXT

BIOGRAPHICAL BACKGROUND

The life and teachings of Socrates (c. 469–399 B.C.) stand at the foundation of Western philosophy. Socrates lived in Athens during a time of transition, as Sparta's defeat of Athens in the Peloponnesian War (431–404 B.C.) ended the Golden Age of Athenian civilization. Socrates himself never recorded his thoughts, so our only record of his life and ideas comes from his contemporaries. These accounts are mixed and often biased by the authors' personal interpretations.

Most of what we know about Socrates comes from the writings of Plato (427–347 B.C.). The child of wealthy and well-connected Athenian parents, Plato was both Socrates' student and Aristotle's teacher. Though seemingly destined to become a politician because of his family's high social status, Plato ultimately shunned the political life. Plato's rejection of politics may have been motivated by two factors. First, following the Peloponnesian War Athens became dominated by a corrupt and wealthy group of citizens. Second, in 399 B.C. this same corrupt government tried, convicted, and executed Socrates. These events caused Plato to call into question and ultimately reject the legitimacy of any government based upon the claim to justice. Though some people believe that Plato may have served the state as a soldier in the war, he firmly turned his back on his state's authority when it clashed with his morals.

Having shunned politics, Plato chose to focus his efforts in the realm of philosophy, assuming a lifelong quest to develop and record the teachings of Socrates. Plato put into writing the style and method of inquiry that Socrates had used in spoken conversation, and developed his own treatments of the investigations that Socrates had begun. Plato's writings, which often take the form of hypothetical dialogues between Socrates and his contemporaries, include studies of ethics, metaphysics, epistemology, justice, politics, and virtue.

Plato's most famous writings focus on ethics. Works such as *Gorgias* and *The Republic* take up a bold stance against evil, greed, and corruption of authority and promote strong new views of virtue and justice. These writings implicitly attack the wealthy and corrupt leadership of Athens at the time. Furthermore, Plato's decision to voice these views through the mouthpiece of the doomed character Socrates instills these texts with an urgent, passionate tone.

In 385 B.C., Plato founded the Academy, an institution devoted to the study of philosophy and mathematics. One purpose of the Academy was to educate a ruling class of "philosopher-kings," which Plato envisions in *The Republic*. The students of the Academy aimed for a pure understanding of truth through the intense application of analytical reason to human life and thought. In operation for approximately nine hundred years, the Academy was an ancestor of the modern university. Due to his role in the establishment of formal higher education and to the vast breadth, impact, and enduring relevance of his ideas, many hold Plato to be the father of Western thought.

HISTORICAL CONTEXT

The problems discussed in *Euthyphro, Apology, Crito,* and *Phaedo* relate closely to the state of Athenian society leading up to Plato's writing of the dialogues. Though classical Greece is often characterized as the epitome of a proper and successful democracy, by the time Plato completed these works the balanced nature of Athenian government had changed considerably. With the end of the Peloponnesian War came a new political authority in Athens, consisting of a group of wealthy, corrupt, and opportunistic citizens more interested in their own prosperity than their society's well being. Not only was the new government corrupt, but its rise to power was anything but smooth and peaceful. Rather, it took place at the conclusion of many years of battle and civil strife, with Athens fast losing hold of its trademark justice and democracy.

Then, in an event that affected Plato deeply and personally, these new rulers tried and executed Socrates, charging him with the very corruption and treason for which the rulers themselves were guilty. The accused Socrates did not attempt to escape or plead for mercy, but rather stated his case and welcomed his death as the virtuous end of a good and just life. This sequence of events, with their murderous conclusion, was devastating for Plato, who was extremely close to his mentor both philosophically and personally. Plato went on to spend much of his life trying to define concepts such as power, justice, truth, and virtue, at least partly in an attempt to reconcile Socrates' virtuous life with his death at the hands of the greedy and corrupt. In this regard, Socrates' execution, along with Socrates' own intense interest in morality during his life, helps explain Plato's attempts to define an objective ethical standard. Plato's treatment of issues such as piety, law, virtue, and death possess great relevance and urgency in light of their close connection to the events taking place at the time. The dialogues embody a philosophy of inquiry and truth that Plato believed necessary for virtue to survive the dark circumstances of his age.

PHILOSOPHICAL CONTEXT

Plato's writings traditionally fall into three categories. The early dialogues—which include *Euthyphro, Apology, Crito,* and *Phaedo*—take the form of conversations in which the character Socrates asks a series of questions. These questions are discussed and resolved as the characters reach a consensus, a format that enables Plato to move through a broad range of philosophical subjects. In these Socratic writings, Plato attempts to capture the essence of his teacher's method and insights. These texts focus on various aspects of ethics and proper living, areas with which Socrates was greatly concerned.

In his subsequent writings, Plato begins to move away from an exclusively Socratic style, most likely because he has already so successfully accomplished his earlier goal of commemorating Socrates' teachings. Plato's middle works, such as *The Republic,* feature more complex, uniquely Platonic tone and subject matter, though Socrates' influence remains clear. Rather than consider strictly ethical matters, Plato pursues other philosophical questions, especially in the realms of metaphysics and epistemology. Though these middle writings maintain the purity of inquiry and pursuit of truth and reason of the earlier texts, they start to apply the traditional approach to a wider array of subjects and questions.

Plato's late dialogues represent the peak of the complexity and diversity that was just beginning in his middle works. These later writings are quite intricate and focus on very specific problems. However, the original, early Socratic themes of ethics and virtue remain important to Plato throughout these later texts.

Despite the differences between Plato's early, middle, and late works, great deal of continuity is present throughout them, as Plato frequently picks up problems he had discussed in earlier works and approaches them from a new perspective. Plato's writings might be thought of as forming a continuous spectrum in which each individual piece gains added clarity and value when compared with other manuscripts that consider similar topics—even if each manuscript's conclusions are different. Whereas each individual text studies certain aspects of life, taken as a whole the entire body of writings presents an inclusive, holistic picture of life in general. Perhaps the most important factor unifying Plato's works is his investigation of the nature of virtue. Plato repeatedly attempts to define morality objectively throughout his lifetime, returning again and again to the topic. Consequently, his numerous inquiries into the nature of proper existence combine to create an overall picture of virtue.

The four *Death of Socrates* dialogues epitomize Socratic exploration of various topics, including religion, law, virtue, and truth. These dialogues' basic insights arise from specific questions, such as what makes something holy, what makes someone properly pious, and so on. General definitions evolve from more specific considerations, just as the general themes of Platonic philosophy evolve from specific texts. Furthermore, the dialogues contain certain fundamental Socratic attributes. In his trademark gesture, the character of Socrates repeatedly professes his own ignorance throughout the texts, and the dialogues often end not with absolute conclusions but with an acknowledgment that they are deficient in wholly explaining the topics in question. Given the close relation between these dialogues and the historical events of Socrates' trial and execution, this inconclusiveness should come as no surprise. Plato wishes to vindicate the memory of his mentor against Socrates' conviction and execution, and one approach is to show the inconclusiveness of even seemingly expert human understanding regarding matters of right and wrong. Thus, these four dialogues both offer a portrait of Socrates and provide the basis for his defense. As such, the dialogues maintain philosophical as well as historical significance.

OVERVIEW

EUTHYPHRO

Euthyphro opens at the entrance to the Athenian law courts, with Euthyphro asking Socrates what he is doing there. Socrates explains that a young man named Meletus has brought charges of corruption and impiety against him and that consequently he is now under indictment. Euthyphro himself is at court because of a murder charge he has brought against his own father.

Socrates expresses surprise upon hearing of Euthyphro's case. He remarks that Euthyphro must possess vast knowledge of divine matters in order to assume that prosecuting his father is the right thing to do. Euthyphro calmly asserts that he knows all about what is holy and what is unholy, and that his wisdom distinguishes him from the common run of men. Socrates therefore requests Euthyphro's instruction regarding the nature of piety so that he might better represent himself during his approaching case against Meletus.

In the discussion that follows, Socrates prods Euthyphro into offering several different definitions of piety and holiness in succession, each of which Socrates easily refutes. First, Euthyphro states that holiness amounts to prosecuting the perpetrators of crimes, especially more serious crimes such as murder or sacrilege. This definition, however, does not satisfy Socrates, as many acts other than prosecution also should count as holy, pious, or lawful. Euthyphro then declares any object or action the gods find pleasing to be holy. In response, Socrates points out that conflicts of opinion are common among the gods, who do not themselves agree about what they find pleasing or distasteful. The same person, object, or action therefore might appear simultaneously holy to some gods and unholy to others. An adequate and stable definition of piety requires something more.

Euthyphro proposes that that which *all* the gods love is holy and pious. In order to consider such a claim, Socrates embarks upon an elaborate discussion of essential versus accidental properties. He concludes that what is holy cannot be identical with what is loved by all the gods, since a thing is loved by the gods *because* it is holy. Holiness determines divine approval, so holiness must be something other than such approval.

Next, Socrates incites Euthyphro to assert that holiness and piety consist of attending to and pleasing the gods. Socrates expresses his puzzlement that omnipotent beings could require any form of "caring for" by mere humans, and the two men go on to consider the nature of the relationship between gods and men. After increasingly intense pressure from Socrates, Euthyphro offers his final suggestion: that piety consists of proper transactions with the gods through rituals, prayer, and sacrifice. Such trading does not in any way aid the gods' existence but instead simply gratifies them.

Socrates points out that to equate holiness with gratification of the gods appears no different from the prior statement that what is holy is that which the gods view with approval. This twist leads to problems already considered, and rather than work them out once more, Euthyphro departs. As a result, the dialogue ends inconclusively.

APOLOGY

The *Apology* presents an account of Socrates' trial for charges of impiety and the corruption of Athenian youths. Far from being an apology in the contemporary sense of an acknowledgment of wrongdoing and expression of contrition, this dialogue's title derives from the Greek word *apologia,* meaning "defense." Plato portrays Socrates as calm, confident, and almost conversational in spite of the potential seriousness of the predicament he faces.

Socrates begins by begging to be excused for his ignorance of judicial matters and proceedings, and he asks those present for their patience and understanding. He makes clear his intentions to speak simply, honestly, and without pretense, and goes on to mention the Oracle at Delphi. This prophet once declared Socrates to be the wisest of all men, but Socrates himself has been unable to discern the precise nature of his own wisdom. He describes his investigations, from which he finally has concluded that his superior knowledge must consist of an awareness of his lack of knowledge—a level of comprehension other humans never reach. Indeed, it is this unique understanding that has set Socrates apart from his countrymen, angering some of them and prompting their charges against him this very day.

Next, Socrates cross-examines his accuser, Meletus, at great length, as permitted by Greek law at the time. Throughout the ensuing dialogue—dominated of course by Socrates—a portrait of the latter's uncompromising virtue and the pure pursuit of truth gradually emerges. Whether or not we are convinced by the arguments

Socrates offers, Plato uses them in an attempt to vindicate Socrates' life, sentencing, and death for posterity.

Socrates' behavior and speech are strikingly unapologetic. He acknowledges that he is a catalyst for Athenian action—stinging the state into action as a fly might provoke a horse. When found guilty, he proposes that his penalty be "free maintenance by the state." He rejects prison or exile as unacceptable options. When he learns that he is sentenced to death rather than assessed a fine, Socrates is unfazed. He attributes his utter lack of distress to an ignorance of death and beyond. Socrates warns his jury that their verdict inflicts harm on themselves and their country rather than upon Socrates himself.

CRITO

Crito takes place in Socrates' prison cell, where the philosopher awaits his impending execution. One day, before dawn, a friend and contemporary named Crito visits Socrates. Crito informs Socrates of arrangements for his escape and attempts to convince Socrates of the desirability of fleeing. Socrates resists the idea of such a flight. This stubbornness, however, leads Crito to mount additional attempts at persuading Socrates to escape with him.

Crito argues that Socrates' execution would cast shame on the philosopher's friends, that he should not fear the expense of fleeing, and that he really might achieve a pleasant life in exile. More significant, Crito argues that Socrates' acceptance of his execution amounts to assisting his enemies in unjustly wronging him. Surely Socrates should deem such implicit support for wrongdoing unacceptable. Furthermore, Crito says that Socrates' two sons will lose their father should he assent to death. Therefore, he must escape his sentence out of concern for his sons' well being.

Socrates replies immediately. He first responds that, as with any issue, public opinion possesses no weight or relevance in the face of wise expert opinion. Furthermore, performance of virtuous actions is much more important than public sentiment. Therefore, only virtue—not popular opinion—should be taken into account when considering what action to perform. All that matters to Socrates is whether or not his escape is a virtuous action.

In order to consider this question, Plato personifies the Laws of Athens, with whom Socrates converses hypothetically throughout the remainder of the dialogue. Essentially, Socrates concludes that to break one law is to break the entire set of laws, since together they comprise one integrated entity. Just as a child should not strike a parent, a citizen should not reject his country's laws but instead may attempt only to persuade the law to free him.

Put differently, Socrates reasons that because he has willingly consented to live in Athens for approximately seventy years, he has chosen to accept its laws. To flee from and thereby reject the laws now would oppose both reason and virtue. As a result, Socrates refuses this option. *Crito* concludes with Socrates' acceptance of his imminent death both convincing and mystifying his longtime friend.

PHAEDO

Just prior to Socrates' execution, several of Socrates' friends, students, and admirers have begun to gather regularly in their mentor's prison cell in order to pass the days in conversation. Among them are Socrates' old friend Crito and two other philosophers, Simmias and Cebes. When it becomes clear that his execution is quite near, Socrates declares that a wise man welcomes death, though he does not go so far as to take his own life. As a means by which to support such a claim, Socrates offers four arguments for the immortality of souls: from Opposites, Recollection, Affinity, and Forms. Through a detailed debate with Simmias and Cebes, Socrates endeavors to display the nature of life, death, truth, and immortality.

After successfully refuting his friends' objections, Socrates relates to them a myth of dying, calmly drinks his murderous poison, and slips into the afterlife.

TERMS

APOLOGY

Socrates' words before the Court of Athens in Plato's *Apology* are anything but what we would normally think of as apologetic. In fact, the only point at which Socrates excuses himself comes before he addresses the jurors, when he apologizes for his ignorance of judicial proceedings. The dialogue's title instead derives from the Greek word *apologia,* meaning "defense." As was customary in ancient Athens, Socrates must defend himself before the court. The *Apology* represents Plato's attempt to reenact this event.

Throughout his self-defense, Socrates shows neither regret for his actions nor fear of their severe consequences. He maintains that the highest achievement of wisdom one may attain is awareness of the worthlessness of human wisdom, and he attempts to make clear how flawed are Meletus's accusations against him. Ultimately, armed with the belief that considerations of virtue outweigh those of safety, Socrates willingly accepts his death sentence rather than compromise his ethical principles.

Because Socrates—as portrayed by Plato, at least—both successfully justifies his teachings and behaves virtuously regardless of the outcome of his actions, his defense appears victorious in spite of the jurors' guilty verdict.

ARGUMENTS FOR IMMORTALITY

Plato offers four arguments for the immortality of human souls, the topic that is the main focus of Socrates' conversations in the *Phaedo.* Socrates' convictions about his soul's immortality both give him courage and enable him to define virtue (as a lack of regard for all considerations but transcendent goodness). To Socrates, these four arguments conclusively prove that our souls persist after our bodies die. Therefore, in making decisions about how to act, mortal matters such as death should not outweigh considerations, such as virtue, that apply to souls beyond their simply human existence. In order of presentation, the four arguments for the soul's immortality emerge from Opposites, Recollection, Affinity, and the Theory of Forms.

Opposites All things, in some sense, must come to be through their opposites. For example, part of the value of something large results from its relationship to anything small—namely that of being larger than the smaller thing. Thus from smaller comes larger, as from larger comes smaller. This formulation applies to all features of existence. As a result, the opposites of life and death must manifest the same connection: from death comes life, and from life comes death. We are alive now, in a life that inevitably brings death with it. But due to the nature of opposites, this death in turn must be accompanied by further life. In this manner we may know our souls to be immortal.

Recollection As Socrates describes, we might encounter two objects of equal length, for example, a two-inch wire and a two-inch antenna. Our senses reveal to us the perception of their lengths. From these impressions we recognize an abstract concept of equality applying to both objects' lengths but separate from the content of our perception of the objects. For Plato, this recognition implies that beyond the experience of our senses, we possess knowledge about universal properties such as pure length, justice, and beauty. We grasp equality even though nothing about the wire and antenna grants us direct awareness of this ideal form of resemblance. Our bodies access all information through sensation, so any abstract awareness of pure forms implies the recollection of knowledge from an existence of our souls distinct from that of our bodies. For Socrates, this implication provides evidence for our souls' immortality.

Affinity All entities submit to classification as either of two types. One type includes those entities that appear immaterial, invisible, and immortal; the other type includes those that seem corporeal, visible, and mortal. Bodies belong to the second type of existence, while souls fall under the first. As such, souls are immortal.

The Theory of Forms According to Plato's Theory of Forms, everything that we can perceive with our senses is an embodiment of an ideal, abstract form that cannot be directly perceived in itself. Some of the properties of the things we see and feel are accidental properties, such as the particular heat of a given day; others comprise features that are essential to the thing in question, such as the heat of fire. The essential properties of the thing are attributes of the Form. Life appears to be an essential quality of the human soul. People live, and death involves a separation of the body from the soul, after which the body remains dead. Because we do not exhibit vitality independent from our souls upon death, when body separates from soul, our souls must bring life to our bodies. Otherwise, there would be no explanation for our vitality, as neither our bodies nor our souls would cause this vitality. Life therefore appears to be an essential feature of souls. In turn, Plato, through Socrates, asserts the immortality of the soul.

ESSENTIAL VS. ACCIDENTAL PROPERTIES

Though Socrates does not explicitly use the terms "essential" and "accidental," his discussion of piety in *Euthyphro* depends crucially upon a distinction between the essential versus the accidental features of any entity. Heat, for example, is an *essential* property of fire: the two necessarily go hand in hand, and nothing without heat qualifies as flame. On the other hand, red is an *accidental* property of stop signs: it is perfectly conceivable to imagine a blue stop sign so long as the sign retains its essential quality of four letters configured to spell "stop." One cannot, however, conceive of a cold flame.

Socrates uses this distinction to claim that the approval of the gods is an accidental quality of pious entities. The entities' holiness and piety, however, are essential aspects of holy existence. Applying this essential-accidental distinction to considerations of piousness reveals that what is holy must be something fundamentally different from that which is loved by the gods—the former is an essential property of holiness, while the latter is not. This argument debunks Euthyphro's definition of piety.

THE LAWS OF ATHENS

In the *Crito,* Plato personifies the Laws of Athens as a means to emphasize Socrates' virtue and to introduce the notion of a social contract. Thus, even when Socrates' admirers tell him of their arrangements for his flight from execution, he refuses on grounds of propriety: to flee would be to defy virtue. In order to prove such a claim, Socrates imagines a hypothetical conversation between himself and the personification of the Laws, a figure he provides with an almost parental voice. From this conversation Socrates concludes that to flee would be to violate the contract he has entered into with Athens by living in the city voluntarily for so many years. Staying there for so long, Socrates has implicitly accepted the ways and laws of the land. As a result, now he cannot choose to break the laws as he pleases. To do so would be to violate both reason and virtue by opposing his agreement with the state merely due to a fear of death. This perspective reveals Socrates' essential courage and commitment to the good in his actions and teachings. Moreover, it offers a forerunner to the modern philosophical conception of a social contract between a people and their laws.

PIETY

Socrates and Euthyphro spend most of the first *Death of Socrates* dialogue disputing the nature of piety. Though their debate ends inconclusively, it becomes clear from their discussion that piety, or holiness, cannot simply be the prosecution of religious criminals, nor that which all the gods love, nor even those actions that please the gods. A general, overarching definition of piety remains to be formulated by the end of *Euthyphro.* It seems in some sense that Plato might use this inconclusiveness to help paint a picture of Socrates' innocence of allegations impiety, for if no adequate definition of piousness exists, then Socrates cannot be convicted of behaving impiously.

VIRTUE

Considerations of virtue guide Socrates' every action, as he describes in the *Apology.* Essentially, Socrates believes that in all situations and in reflection upon action, considerations of the proper and the good should outweigh any other factors. For this reason, Socrates refuses to avoid his death when doing so requires he somehow compromise his virtue. This theme resurfaces several times throughout the remainder of Socrates' life as depicted by Plato.

CHARACTER LIST

Themes, Ideas & Arguments

Piety

Piety is the central topic of discourse in *Euthyphro*. Socrates and Euthyphro spend most of this dialogue debating back and forth, attempting to define what might be common to all holy acts. Despite this unified focus of their conversation, however, the two men remain unable to formulate any clear, uncontroversial definition of piety. Euthyphro makes several attempts, defining piety as prosecution of civil offenders, as that which is dear to the gods, as that which all the gods approve of or love, and finally as a science of proper transactions with the gods through rituals, reverence, and sacrifice. Socrates, however, quickly dispels each of these formulations, showing that none of them suffice to provide an adequate definition of piety.

This inconclusiveness can be seen as a sort of foreshadowing on Plato's part. In terms of historical context, one of the major charges brought against Socrates—and against which he defends himself in the *Apology*—is impiety. Plato, by presenting us with a detailed analysis of holiness and showing how difficult it is to reach a conclusion on the nature of holiness, in a certain sense vindicates his mentor. Plato shows that Socrates' alleged guilt for impiety might not be so obvious to determine. The culpability simply cannot be clear, as the very nature of the piety Socrates supposedly lacks is indeterminable.

Wisdom

Socrates expresses his famous portrait of wisdom fairly early in the *Apology*. Paradoxically, he believes the greatest human wisdom consists of one's perception of the utter insignificance of human knowledge. Socrates describes his gradual progression toward this conclusion, starting with a declaration by the Oracle at Delphi. The Oracle previously has proclaimed Socrates to be the wisest of all men. Upon hearing these words, Socrates sets out to discover the exact substance of his superior wisdom. He interviews various people, such as poets and craftsmen, in order to learn about his own expertise by listening to how other people know what they know. After perceiving these peoples' lack of true comprehension, Socrates concludes that his own wisdom must consist of an awareness of the general human *lack* of wisdom.

This position does not earn Socrates many friends. Quite the contrary, Socrates' conception of wisdom seems in fact to be largely responsible for his execution. The philosopher attributes the animosity of most of his longtime enemies, as well as their allegations against him, to his view. Socrates finds himself on trial and ultimately convicted because of his refusal to rescind his belief. He dies, then, both because of and in spite of his wisdom.

VIRTUE

Virtue plays a major role in Socrates' execution, though not due to his definition of it. As Socrates spells out in the *Apology,* true pursuers of virtue choose actions according *entirely* to the merit of each given decision. Considerations such as fame, fortune, and—most important—death should not weigh into the decision of how to act in any situation. For this reason, Socrates refuses to cease teaching the principles for which he has received an indictment, as to do so would be to sacrifice the proper course of action for the safe one. Such a decision would not manifest virtue and as such should be forbidden. Furthermore, Socrates' commitment to virtue regardless of mortal adversity—resulting from considerations, like those in the *Phaedo,* of the soul's immortality—keeps him from fleeing his execution when the opportunity arises. In this fashion, Socrates' virtue, like his conception of wisdom, helps guarantee his death.

LAW

Plato's decision to personify the Laws of Athens emphasizes the significance Socrates wishes to place on the concept of law. Most humans would likely leap at the chance to escape an impending death sentence, as such a tendency simply emerges from a natural instinct for survival. Yet Socrates overcomes this frailty because of his commitment to law. As he describes, by choosing to live in Athens for so long, he has entered into an agreement. For seventy years Socrates has gladly accepted Athenian customs and society, and to flee now would be to reject this structure and to dishonor his contract with its law. One cannot adopt and abandon laws at one's convenience, as such behavior undermines the very nature of the laws—that of a voluntary contract between the laws and the citizens living under them. For this reason, Socrates holds that a logical, virtuous commitment to the law requires complete submission to any of the law's proclamations. Such is the case even if the law mandates one face execution as a consequence of virtuous actions, as it does in Socrates' case.

IMMORTALITY

Much of the *Phaedo* focuses on the immortality of souls. It gradually becomes clear that Socrates' ideas about what happens *after* this life inform his beliefs regarding what should take place *during* this life. In order to demonstrate the soul's persistence beyond any particular body, Socrates employs arguments from Opposites, Recollections, and Affinity, as well as a prototypical account of Plato's Theory of Forms. Respectively, these formulations convey that life must occur from death if death also occurs from life; that our senses cause us to recollect knowledge we could have obtained only prior to birth; that our souls are of the type of things that typically manifest immortality; and that life is an essential, inevitable property of souls, just as heat is of fire. Each of these arguments points to an immortal aspect of all people—the soul.

Whether or not one accepts Socrates' view of immortality, it is undeniable that his lack of regard for death—and for that matter the very courage of all his convictions—entirely stem from his view of immortality. With his opinion as it is, Socrates becomes able to downplay any harm that might befall him in his current lifetime, for, because of his soul's immortality, what truly matters is virtue *in spite of* considerations specific to one's bodily, human lifetime. In this manner, the views of immortality Socrates expresses in the *Phaedo* are fundamental in explaining his actions while alive as well as to his willingness to die.

DEATH

Death comprises a more abstract theme of the *Phaedo*. Socrates, inspired by his four-pronged proof of immortality, concludes these dialogues with a myth of the afterlife. Within this story, he recounts precise details of the heightened awareness and pure knowledge awaiting some wise and virtuous humans beyond this world. Because Socrates feels that such access to the true essence of reality awaits him, he in a sense looks forward to his execution. Unfortunately, the same cannot be said of his students, friends, and family.

Plato's use of philosophy in considering the nature of death emerges as a striking aspect of the *Phaedo*. The last of Plato's early writings, this dialogue reveals the increased maturity and independence of his voice, although Socrates remains Plato's central mouthpiece. Socrates thus progresses from his professions of ignorance about death and the afterlife in the *Apology* to his detailed account of these aspects of existence in the *Phaedo*. By the time of Socrates' death, Plato depicts his teacher as both knowledgeable about and ready for death.

DEATH

SUMMARY & ANALYSIS

EUTHYPHRO, 2A–5C

> NOTE: *Plato did not divide his writing into sections, so his texts exist as continuous discussions without breaks. This study guide has made artificial divisions corresponding to shifts in topic within each dialogue. Because page numbers may vary in various editions of the text, passages are referenced using the Stephanus page numbers (from a complete medieval edition of Plato's works). As this is the standard system for citing Plato, many editions include the Stephanus notation in their margins.*

SUMMARY

The dialogue commences as Socrates encounters Euthyphro, a fellow Athenian, on the porch of King Archon, a religious magistrate. Euthyphro seems surprised at Socrates' presence near court, and he inquires into the nature of the philosopher's business there. Socrates explains that he is under indictment, facing accusations brought against him by a young man named Meletus. Socrates provides a brief, unfavorable physical description of the prosecutor. He says that he is charged with corrupting Athenian youth and with impiety—inventing new gods while refusing to acknowledge old ones. Despite the serious nature of these allegations, Socrates ironically declares that he shares Meletus's concern for the city's young. Euthyphro mentions the potential connection between Socrates' case and his claims to frequent visitation by supernatural entities. Euthyphro goes on to express empathy for Socrates' troubles.

Socrates then asks Euthyphro why he has come to court, and the younger man replies that he is there regarding a trial for a charge of murder he has brought against his own father. Apparently, in punishing a hired hand for the killing of a servant, Euthyphro's father accidentally caused the hired hand's death—a crime for which Euthyphro wishes to try his father in court. This decision to press charges shocks Socrates, implying that he believes Euthyphro's actions against his parent to be questionable. Euthyphro, however, maintains that the only important consideration in such a situation is lawfulness—issues such as family ties should not affect moral deliberation. Moreover, one who knowingly associates with criminals and does not prosecute them shares equally in their guilt. Euthyphro does admit, though, that his relatives have turned against him since he brought the charges in question.

Socrates remarks that Euthyphro must possess vast knowledge of piety and law to make these detailed claims so confidently, or even to bring this case against his own father in the first place. Surely no one would act in such a fashion unless he could be absolutely sure of the virtuousness of his action. Euthyphro assents to this assertion, declaring his vast knowledge of divine affairs exactly to be the feature that distinguishes himself from other people.

Upon hearing these words, Socrates immediately requests that Euthyphro take him on as a student that so Socrates may better equip himself for his defense against Meletus. Apparently, the philosopher is eager to establish any credibility possible. Since Euthyphro so clearly maintains his ethical expertise, Socrates reflects that Meletus might dismiss the case against him at the very mention of his recent instructions at the hands of such an expert as Euthyphro. Though it is somewhat unclear whether or not Plato intends the words to be sarcastic, Socrates repeats his belief that Euthyphro's instruction might greatly aid his case.

ANALYSIS

Euthyphro's introduction follows the typical pattern of a Socratic dialogue. The conversations in these dialogues generally involve two participants: typically Socrates, who acts as Plato's mouthpiece, and someone else—in this case Euthyphro—who claims some form of excellence or expertise. Socrates employs an inquisitive style of reasoning in which he simply questions his opponents about their arguments. Socrates made this interrogative approach to philosophy famous, and as we learn in the *Apology*, his method of inquiry depends upon the wisdom of a specific form of ignorance. Socrates comes closer to the truth than his interlocutors because he is able to acknowledge what he *does not* know. Though we eventually realize Socrates is wiser than his opponents, he usually begins an argument by professing his lack of knowledge about a given topic and asking the other person to instruct him.

This dialogue presents us with an excellent example of Socrates' standard technique, as Socrates professes from the outset that he does not have sufficient knowledge of piety and that he would like Euthyphro to teach him. Socrates' request that Euthyphro instruct him about holiness is prompted by Euthyphro's audacious prosecution of his own father—an act that implies that Euthyphro has such a thorough understanding of piety that he feels comfortable turning against his own parent without risking offending the gods. Euthyphro, prodded by Socrates, confirms that he thinks himself an expert on piety, confident in his ability to tell right from wrong. Socrates seems to take Euthyphro's assertions at face value, but we can sense at least a hint of irony here, an expectation that the arrogant Euthyphro is setting himself up for a fall.

Euthyphro is important not only as a statement of Plato's early philosophy, but also as a record of historical events. Together, the four *Death of Socrates* dialogues offer both an account of Socrates' teachings and an interpretation of his personality and his actions, relating for posterity the nature of his execution. In Plato's dialogues Socrates' eloquent words offer an implicit self-defense, as his arguments show exactly how his accusers' actions—rather than his own—defy virtue. Plato uses his early writings in an attempt to vindicate Socrates' life, teachings, and death.

EUTHYPHRO, 5 D – 9 E

SUMMARY

Socrates asks Euthyphro to start by teaching him the definitions of piety and impiety. Euthyphro obliges Socrates' request, asserting that piety is the punishment of wrongdoers through judicial prosecution. One may act piously, then, by maintaining vigilant security and exacting retribution from criminals. Conversely, by this definition, impiety equates with the failure to prosecute criminals. Euthyphro refers to myths about the gods Zeus and Kronos punishing their respective fathers, Kronos and Uranus. If Zeus, the most righteous of gods, may prosecute his parent, then surely he, Euthyphro, should not be scorned for a similar action.

Socrates demands to know whether or not Euthyphro believes mythology literally, and Euthyphro responds that he does. Socrates then objects that Euthyphro's definition of piety is only partially adequate. Though Socrates agrees that prosecuting wrongdoers exhibits some level of piety, he points out that other actions or entities may also be classified as holy. Defining piety exclusively as the punishment of criminals thus misses a whole range of situations that should count as pious.

Instead, Socrates requests Euthyphro to formulate a definition capturing some more general, abstract property comprising all holy aspects of existence. Socrates challenges Euthyphro to come up with a pattern or template such that anything that matches it is pious, whereas anything that does not is impious. To this end, Euthyphro attempts a revised definition of piety, saying that piety is that which the gods find agreeable, whereas impiety is that which the gods find disagreeable. Socrates receives Euthyphro's revised definition with far greater hospitality, as it matches the abstract form Socrates desires.

Nonetheless, Socrates quickly undercuts Euthyphro's second definition of piety as well. He reminds Euthyphro of the latter's literal acceptance of mythology and notes that the gods constantly dispute among themselves about what pleases them. Socrates reasons that these disputes must mean that the gods do not agree about what they love. Under Euthyphro's definition of piety, this lack of consensus allows something to exist as both pious and impious. These considerations make Euthyphro's definition imprecise, so something other than the gods' love must comprise piety.

Euthyphro counters that the gods all would agree on the impiety of an unjustified murder. Thus, some actions clearly qualify for unanimous divine disapproval. Socrates does not argue with this point. Instead, he points out that the gods—as well as humans—do not tend to debate about whether or not wrongdoers deserve prosecution. More frequently they debate about whether a given person is or is not guilty of wrongdoing. Some gods might feel that a certain act was just, while others believe the opposite to be true.

As a result, Socrates presses Euthyphro yet further in the search for an adequate definition, causing the younger man to posit that piety amounts to what *all* the gods love.

ANALYSIS

This section further presents Socrates' characteristic approach to philosophy, as he doggedly questions Euthyphro in an attempt to make Euthyphro define his terms. Socrates displays a personality that is eager and curious—qualities he continues to embody throughout these four dialogues. The conversation here helps convey a portrait of Socrates prior to his execution.

Plato's Theory of Forms provides the key for us to understand what Socrates is looking for in his debate with Euthyphro. Essentially, forms embody the purest existence of any properties. All objects or beings that display any quality do so only inasmuch as they partake of the forms' nature. For example, the sky is blue inasmuch as it partakes in the form of blue, something is hot inasmuch as it partakes in the form of heat, and so on for all characteristics of anything. Socrates in essence desires that Euthyphro define the form of piety rather than mere instances of something's participation in piety. For this reason. Socrates repeatedly demands an overarching, universal definition of holiness. Euthyphro's newer definition of piety moves toward the type of general formulation Socrates seeks to describe the form, or basic nature, of piety. That which the gods love includes a far greater range of possible constituents than Euthyphro's earlier, more general version of holiness.

At the same time, Euthyphro's revised definition of piety still does not suffice. Socrates' question about Euthyphro's belief in mythology foreshadows this problem. Euthyphro has already referred to myths about Zeus, Kronos, and Uranus, as well as to his literal belief in mythological events. In effect, Euthyphro succumbs to a trap of his own creation: the gods do not often agree; mythology is a catalog of their intense disagreements. From this fact it follows that piousness must be separate from that which the gods love. The gods disagree about what they love, but any satisfactory definition of piety must avoid such dissent.

Given the close relationship between these dialogues and Socrates' execution, the vagueness of the concept of piety is significant. Socrates dies, at least in part, for what some Athenians perceive to be his impiety. By showing how difficult it is to define piety, Plato demonstrates the flimsiness of the charge levied against Socrates. In this detailed inquiry into the nature of holiness, and in showing the difficulty of such an attempt, Plato subtly undermines the credibility and authority of the charges that led to Socrates' trial and execution.

EUTHYPHRO, 10A–16A

SUMMARY

> "[W]hat is pious is loved [by the gods] because it is
> pious, and not pious because it is loved."
> *(See* QUOTATIONS *, p. 53)*

Socrates demonstrates that Euthyphro's third definition of holiness—that whatever all the gods love is holy—cannot be correct by pointing out that the gods love holy things because they are holy, the things aren't holy because the gods love them. On the other hand, whatever the gods love is loved because they love it—it wouldn't make sense to say that the gods love things because the things are loved. Therefore, being holy and being loved must be two different things.

At this point, Euthyphro expresses his frustration with Socrates, accusing Socrates of distorting words beyond recognition, derailing the momentum of discussion. Socrates answers that he does not intentionally cause such problems, but means only to pursue any line of thought to the logical conclusions it may entail. If anything, Socrates maintains, it is Euthyphro's nebulous ideas that deserve blame.

Socrates steers the debate in a new direction by proposing that everything pious is morally correct, but not everything morally correct is pious. In other words, piety is a subset of moral virtue, the larger category. From the fact that all moral virtue does not count as piety, it follows that piety comprises only one type of moral virtue. Socrates stops at this point to ask Euthyphro to define more specifically what type of virtue piety is. All the while, Socrates continues to praise Euthyphro's great expertise regarding matters of holiness, citing how useful Euthyphro's wisdom will be when Socrates defends himself against Meletus.

Euthyphro answers that piety is the aspect of virtue concerned with attending to the gods. Socrates immediately puzzles over this suggestion, as most interpretations of the concept "attending to," such as that of a trainer attending to a horse, imply some benefit conferred upon the recipient of attention. Supposedly, the gods are omnipotent. As such, the idea of their receiving assistance from any other beings, especially mortal humans, is absurd.

Euthyphro again amends his words, instead asserting that piety resembles a relationship between gods and pious people similar to that between masters and obedient slaves. But this argument runs into the same problem stemming from the gods' omnipotence, so Euthyphro reluctantly moves on to argue that piety consists of a science of pleasing the gods through proper prayer and sacrifice. By this definition, piety equates to the art of commerce between humans and the gods. Because such transactions gratify the gods, they embody piety.

Socrates points out that this definition reduces holiness to that which is dear to the gods—a position Socrates has already refuted. At this point, Euthyphro's frustration becomes too great for him to endure. He departs, and the dialogue ends inconclusively.

Analysis

Socrates' arguments in this section center on the distinction between essential and accidental properties of any object or being. An entity's essential qualities are its absolutely indispensable aspects. Heat, for example, is an essential feature of fire; cold is an essential feature of snow; and wetness is an essential feature of water. One cannot remove these properties without significantly altering the entities they help to comprise. Fire ceases to be fire without heat, so heat is an essential property of fire. Accidental qualities, on the other hand, are not constitutive of the objects that manifest them. Orange, for example, embodies an accidental property of flames, because flames remain flames whether or not their color shifts to blue. For these reasons, such nondefinitive features count as accidental.

Socrates' objection to defining piety as what the gods love is based on this distinction between the essential and the accidental. Socrates insists that the gods' love is an accidental feature of piety. The gods love certain things because the things are holy—not the other way around. Removal of this love would not rid the things of their piety, because such love does not appear essential to holiness. Socrates therefore desires an account of some essential property of holiness, without which nothing is pious. As such, this distinction between accidental and essential features clarifies the problems with Euthyphro's depiction of piety's fundamental nature.

Euthyphro's frustration throughout the dialogue highlights the irony of the roles he and Socrates play within this conversation. At the beginning of the conversation, Socrates eagerly requests that Euthyphro take him on as a pupil, as the younger man claims to have a superior knowledge of piety. In fact, Socrates has spent most of his seventy years teaching by the time he becomes Euthyphro's pupil. Furthermore, toward the end of the dialogue Euthyphro all but abandons his attempts to clarify what makes an object or action holy. Socrates, though supposedly the student, takes hold of the debate because Euthyphro is unable to answer his questions satisfactorily. As a teacher, Euthyphro is clearly a failure. By repeatedly returning to Socrates' stated role as Euthyphro's pupil, Plato uses irony to underscore that it is in fact Socrates, not Euthyphro, who plays the role of true teacher.

This pattern is common within Plato's early dialogues: Socrates' interlocutors often initially claim some type of expertise and ability to instruct Socrates, but then ultimately receive Socrates' instruction on the topic rather than provide him with their own. Socrates' approach to philosophy, which consists almost entirely of asking questions, frequently frustrates those with whom he disputes.

What Plato ultimately accomplishes with the *Euthyphro* is to suggest how ambiguous the concept of piety really is, thereby calling into question Socrates' supposed impiety. He does this by having Socrates repeatedly push the conversation past the point where Euthyphro can claim to know what he is talking about. The inconclusiveness of the debate suggests that it may actually be impossible to adequately define the nature of piety, even with such a rigorous inquiry into the issue as transpires in this dialogue.

APOLOGY, 17A–23C

SUMMARY

> "The wisest of you men is he who has realized, like
> Socrates, that in respect of wisdom he is really
> worthless." *(See* QUOTATIONS *, p. 54)*

Socrates opens his case with an appeal to the jury to listen to him with an open mind. His accusers have already spoken against him in the flowery manner common in courts of law and have warned the jury not to be deceived by Socrates, a skillful speaker. Socrates immediately addresses himself to that issue, claiming that while his accusers' speeches contained great refinement and skill, he lacks the ability to speak so well. However, he remarks, he will speak the truth, whereas his opponents uttered only falsehood.

Socrates apologizes for his own verbal ineptitude. He mentions that he has never appeared before a court and therefore excuses himself because of his lack of judicial experience. He hopes his commitment to the truth will outweigh such inexperience with the law. Socrates also reveals that his words are entirely unprepared. This spontaneity contrasts with the practiced deliveries of his opponents. Next, Socrates asks the jury's forgiveness should he slip into his more common conversational style. Finally, he requests that the court consider only whether or not his case is just rather than how well he presents it.

Socrates goes on to assert that the current prosecutors—Meletus, Anytus, and Lycon—are only the most recent group of his detractors. More dangerous are his plethora of longtime accusers, as they have been spreading the word about Socrates' supposed evil and atheism since they were children. Furthermore, these antagonists remain virtually unknown, except for the dramatist Aristophanes (whose play *The Clouds* satirizes Socrates). As such, they cannot submit to cross-examination regarding their position. Socrates therefore may only infer his detractors' claims from the charges against him—that he does not believe in the gods, but instead formulates physical explanations for phenomena, and that he instructs others how to overcome stronger arguments with weaker ones through the skillful use of rhetoric.

Socrates begins his defense by declaring his lack of interest and expertise in matters of the gods and natural causes. He goes on to contrast himself with rhetoricians, such as the Sophists, who charge fees for their teachings. These men teach their students how to twist words and arguments, and in return receive money for their time, whereas Socrates does neither—as any Athenian could attest, given Socrates' impoverished state. Instead, Socrates declares his own ignorance and consequent inability to charge for teaching. He believes he has been falsely accused simply due to the extraordinary nature of his ways and ideas.

In an effort to account for his reputation, Socrates describes the series of events through which he discovered his own wisdom. The Oracle at Delphi, a divine authority, proclaimed to Socrates' friend Chaerephon that Socrates is the wisest of all humans. Upon hearing these words, Socrates set out to determine the Oracle's exact meaning, seeking to know what might comprise his wisdom. After interviewing many supposed experts, such as politicians, poets, and craftsmen, Socrates became increasingly aware of the limited nature of their specific expertise. Despite the unpopularity of this view, Socrates began to surmise that most people, especially self-proclaimed experts, significantly lack practical knowledge. Rather than oppose the Oracle's decree, Socrates concludes that his great wisdom must consist of his ability to perceive the *absence* of knowledge. For this reason, Socrates has devoted his life to teaching others of their ignorance, as his own knowledge of such affairs is exactly what renders him so wise in the eyes of the gods. In short, Socrates believes the complaints against him to be based upon his simple doctrine of human ignorance.

ANALYSIS

Given this dialogue's title, it may seem striking to us that Socrates apologizes for very little. In fact, the philosopher's mention of his inexperience with judicial proceedings is the only apology—in the conventional sense—he provides. This apparent contradiction, however, is resolved through the title's derivation 'from the Greek word *apologia*, or "defense." Ancient Greek law dictated that defendants maintained the right—and responsibility—to defend themselves. In order to accomplish this defense, each person facing charges pleaded his case before court, regardless of prior experience with matters of law.

By contrasting the studied, artificial—and false—speech of his accusers with his own improvised, conversational, truthful speech, Socrates distinguishes himself not only from his opponents but also from the Sophists, a group of professional teachers who instructed the wealthy youth of Athens in oratory. Throughout his works, Plato paints an unflattering picture of the Sophists as shallow thinkers who taught young men to overcome sound reasoning with shoddy reasoning by means of rhetoric. Socrates has often been mistakenly classed with these Sophists, whom he despises. The speech of his accusers is influenced by the Sophists, who have taught them to speak convincingly and yet falsely. By contrasting himself with these men, Socrates at once invokes the common prejudice against sophistry against his accusers and distances himself from their practices. He remarks that he is only a skillful speaker if by "skillful speaker" is meant someone who speaks the truth.

Socrates' insistence that he lacks any kind of expertise in any field whatsoever is central to his philosophy, and it sets him apart from both the Sophists and the Presocratic philosophers. Teachers from these two groups both claimed that through experience, inspiration, or investigation, they had gained access to special knowledge that could be taught. Socrates, on the other hand, never makes any particular claims to knowledge, and his inquiries tend to show the ignorance of his interlocutors rather than his own expertise. Socrates, then, has no particular knowledge, as such, to teach at all, but has instead a peculiar kind of wisdom that will be clarified in the sections following.

The oracle of Apollo at Delphi was the most famous and revered oracle of the ancient world. That Socrates' friend Chaerephon did in fact visit the oracle is confirmed by Xenophon, though in his account the oracle declared Socrates to be "the most free, upright, and prudent of all people" (Xenophon, *Socrates' Defense*) rather than the most wise. In either case, it is clear that the oracle made a positive claim about Socrates. Most of Plato's early dialogues—those that center more on Socrates' thought than on Plato's own—are concerned with ethical questions, and so we can perhaps reconcile Xenophon's and Plato's accounts by saying that Socrates' wisdom is a kind of ethical wisdom, one that would make him supremely free, upright, and prudent. However, the Delphic oracle sided primarily with Sparta during the Peloponnesian War, so it is doubtful whether an Athenian jury would trust or appreciate the evidence given by the oracle.

Also of relevance is the famous motto inscribed above the entrance to the oracle at Delphi: "Know thyself." Socrates is an ardent advocate of self-knowledge, and his investigations can be seen as an attempt to come to a better understanding of his own nature. He is famous for claiming that no one could ever knowingly and willingly do evil, that evil is a result of ignorance and deficient self-knowledge. His investigations generally ask such questions as what it is to be virtuous, or pious, or just. In his dogged efforts to understand these terms himself, and his persistence in showing his interlocutors to be wrong in assuming they have such understanding, Socrates reveals himself as a man intent on gaining the self-knowledge necessary to lead a virtuous life.

APOLOGY, 23C–34B

SUMMARY

> "[A man] has only one thing to consider in performing
> any action; that is, whether he is acting rightly or
> wrongly, like a good man or a bad one."
> *(See* QUOTATIONS *, p. 55)*

Having sufficiently addressed the charges of his longtime accusers, Socrates continues by refuting the allegations Meletus has brought. Socrates reminds the court of the two main indictments against his actions: that he corrupts the minds of youths and that he invents his own gods rather than acknowledging those of the state.

Socrates questions Meletus, asking him who has a good influence on the young. Meletus replies that the laws influence youth positively. Socrates counters that he would like Meletus to name specific people, rather than things, who have had good influence. Socrates further prods Meletus to specify those people whose business it is to know the laws and who have this positive impact. Meletus offers jurymen, benefactors, members of the council, and assemblymen as examples. As any adult male may take part in the assembly, it follows that essentially every Athenian has a positive influence on the young.

At this point, Socrates marvels that he himself, of all Athenians, should be singled out as a sole corrupter of youth. He draws an analogy to horses and horse training, meant to imply that only a few specialists improve children, while most people have merely a neutral impact on them—just as with horses.

Meletus accuses Socrates of intentionally harming his fellow citizens, to which Socrates replies that he himself suffers from wickedness directed toward others, for he shares society with these people. As such, he has no desire intentionally to wrong them, so either he has not done so or has done so only unknowingly. Moreover, if the latter is the case, Socrates deserves not punishment but instruction.

Meletus asserts that Socrates teaches the young to believe in gods of his own invention and that Socrates himself does not believe in any gods at all. Socrates mocks this line of attack, pointing out that in order to discuss the activity of any entity, such as a horse, a man, or a piece of music, one must believe in the existence of the thing in question—horses, human beings, or music. By this token, as Socrates speaks of supernatural activities, he must believe in supernatural beings. Because all supernatural beings are gods or their children, Meletus's charge that Socrates does not believe in any gods amounts to a false one.

Next, Socrates reflects aloud that some might wonder whether he feels ashamed to have chosen a way of life that increases his risk of death. He quickly justifies his decision by stating that only considerations of right and wrong, not of physical safety, matter in choosing an action. In addition, Socrates believes that abandoning philosophy in the face of death amounts to disobeying the divine command of Apollo himself. He also argues that fear of death equates to false knowledge of matters that remain beyond human accessibility. These words echo Socrates' claims to a special wisdom of ignorance.

In light of these considerations, Socrates explains that nothing will stop him from performing his divinely ordained duty to show fellow humans their ignorance—even a penalty of death. Furthermore, Socrates maintains that the members of the jury, in ordering his execution, do more harm to themselves than to him. It is far worse to commit a wrong act, such as the killing of an innocent man, than it is to remain good and suffer from the wrongdoing of others. Socrates believes that dying innocently at the hands of his jury is far more just than wrongly sentencing someone else to death. He likens himself to a fly stinging a sleeping horse (Athens) into action. He predicts that he will be missed after his death and that he eventually will be recognized as the catalyst for an Athenian awakening.

Finally, Socrates attributes his persistent teachings to a supernatural voice that guides him. He justifies his solitary life as necessary to one who opposes the impure politics of society, and he refers to multiple civic occasions on which he has demonstrated virtue in the face of adversity. Socrates claims that he owes his survival in the face of opposition entirely to this divine voice. He reiterates his commitment to justice and obedience of the gods, mentions several men present—including Plato—who could attest to his virtue, and concludes that Meletus's charges must be false.

ANALYSIS

Socrates' words embody the essence of his lifelong intellectual outlook, making the *Apology* a masterful biographical portrait. The strongest example of this portraiture comes when Socrates declares that a man "has only one thing to consider in performing any action; that is, whether he is acting rightly or wrongly, like a good man or a bad one." Socrates uses this claim to justify his own decision to continue teaching regardless of the enemies this practice earns him. Though Socrates' choice puts him at risk of death, its virtuousness is the only important factor in his reflection. His belief in the importance of righteousness over all other factors stems from his conceptions of virtue, wisdom, the soul, and its afterlife—the major points of focus of his intellectual inquiry. By integrating these key tenets of Socrates' philosophy into the account of his self-defense, Plato highlights his mentor's essential philosophical doctrines for the historical record.

The different strands of history, biography, and philosophy that run through this dialogue are woven together when Socrates mentions Plato's presence at the trial. This reference emphasizes Plato's role as creator of the *Apology* and represents an attempt on Plato's part to lend himself credibility as a firsthand witness to the proceedings he recounts. We are meant to trust Plato's words more because he is actually present when Socrates speaks them. Whether or not we accept Plato's account as unbiased, it is one of the only thorough sources of information regarding the events surrounding Socrates' death. More important, though, only Plato possesses the philosophical, personal, and historical access to Socrates necessary for a portrayal as robust as he gives us in these dialogues.

Socrates' predictions regarding the impact of his death upon Athenian society contrast with his other words throughout the *Apology*. These statements reflect Plato's desire to register the nature and impact of Socrates' death—Plato's explicit purpose in creating these dialogues. At the same time, it is debatable whether Socrates was correct in his prediction that he would awaken Athens. Socrates seems to contradict himself somewhat, stating both that he cannot be replaced and that other critics soon will replace him. As such, the dialogue does not render his meaning entirely clear. Furthermore, accepting the idea that Socrates suffers less harm than his executioners requires that we accept his philosophy. If we deny this belief in virtue before death, we may also deny that Socrates' jurors suffer the greater evil for killing him than he does by dying unjustly at their hands.

APOLOGY, 34B–42A

SUMMARY

After completing his defense, Socrates admits his concern that the jurors will sentence him to a more severe punishment in light of his refusal to beg for their mercy. He mentions his own children, emphasizing that he has no desire to bring them before the court in a bid for pity or to beg for his acquittal. Socrates feels that such actions would defy the reputation and principles he has established throughout the course of his lifetime. He has no desire to disgrace himself or his city, as he believes no self-respecting virtuous individual like himself would.

Socrates takes this position because unrighteousness brings with it the risk of eternal condemnation. Moreover, in attempting to convince the jury, he wishes to rely only upon his arguments rather than desperate pleas for clemency. Socrates maintains that the court itself, in the interests of justice and piety, should desire he not behave in such an immoral manner. For these reasons, Socrates declares himself to be more sincere and interested in the truth than are his accusers.

Upon learning of the jurors' guilty verdict, Socrates is not surprised at the outcome—in fact, he seems surprised only by the vote's narrow margin. Though he feels he has revealed his own innocence regardless of the court's decision, he also concedes that he must address Meletus's request for the death penalty. In fact, Socrates must suggest what he himself believes to be a reasonable punishment.

Socrates mentions the service he has performed for his fellow citizens: attempting to persuade them individually to focus on spiritual rather than practical well-being. As the verdict against him stems from his attempts to accomplish this magnanimous goal, he feels that a life supported by the state would be the most appropriate "punishment" for him. To support this proposal, Socrates adds that never in his life has he deliberately wronged another person, whether or not his jurors believe such a claim. He flatly refuses punishments of fines and exile, asserting that he will not cling to life so desperately as to compromise his principles with such plea-bargaining. Furthermore, Socrates remains unwilling to cease his teachings, as doing so would disobey the will of the gods—itself a truly impious action. Consequently, neither fine nor banishment will keep him out of the type of trouble he currently faces, as such predicaments emerge from the instruction he refuses to cease. Besides, Socrates has no money to speak of anyway.

Upon hearing the court's sentence of death, Socrates mockingly replies that he soon would have died naturally anyway. He reflects that the verdict follows from his unwillingness to say what his jurors want to hear. He again asserts that he would rather die from a defense that docs not compromise his principles than live by one that does. Socrates compares his situation to instances of bravery in war, expressing satisfaction that he faces only death, whereas his prosecutors are condemned to wickedness. He thus predicts that a terrible vengeance will befall his prosecutors and those who convict him.

Socrates goes on to address those jurors who have voted to acquit him—his "friends." He mentions that the voice that guides his actions when he wanders astray has remained silent throughout his trial. For Socrates, this absence speaks conclusively to the beneficial nature of that which awaits him in this world and others. He knows that had he been heading down a path of danger and unvirtuous action, his supernatural ally would have corrected his direction. The voice has not spoken to him, so Socrates believes the events taking place to be for the best—fate playing itself out properly. In fact, Socrates expresses his excitement at the prospect of dying. He hints at his uncertainty about the nature of death, reiterates that no harm can come to a good person, asks that his contemporaries keep his children on the path of virtue, and calmly accepts his approaching execution.

ANALYSIS

In Socrates' words in this final section of the *Apology,* Plato paints a vivid picture of the uncompromising virtue with which his mentor lived and that led to his eventual execution. On the most literal level, this righteousness explains Socrates' refusal to beg for the mercy of the court or to create an emotional scene that might persuade the jurors to absolve him of guilt. Upon closer consideration, however, Socrates' intentions are not as straightforward. He mentions his children, for example, as instances of the kind of heart-wrenching personal details he does not wish to employ. Yet by the very content of such a statement Socrates performs just what he declares he will not attempt. In other words, he appeals to this cause for sympathy in order to emphasize his intentions not to appeal to such causes for sympathy. This inherently contradictory assertion renders Socrates' actual intent somewhat unclear.

In spite of this particular inconsistency, the remainder of the *Apology* reaffirms Socrates' commitment to virtue above all else. The most obvious example of this focus comes with Socrates' recognition that his death sentence results directly from the nature of his defense. More specifically, Socrates acknowledges he would rather die knowing he has defended himself according to principles of virtue than live simply because he was willing to compromise these principles. This position embodies the quintessential feature of Socrates' doctrine of ethics: considerations of virtue outweigh all other factors in any given situation. In a sense, his assertion that he could have avoided death but has chosen not to represents the philosophical climax of these four dialogues.

Socrates displays a great open-mindedness toward the afterlife, even going so far as to welcome the prospect of dying—a seemingly irrational move that he soon explains. This portion of the *Apology* represents perhaps Plato's most concerted and concise effort to convey the essence of Socrates' philosophy and style. Virtue—with its focus on questions of justice, morality, and virtuous action—was the primary major focus of Socrates' lifelong inquiry. By having Socrates state that he consciously chooses his fate in the name of virtue, Plato effectively depicts the nature of Socrates' convictions and the faithfulness with which he adhered to them. Moreover, this portion of the *Apology* also captures the essence of Socrates' style through its ongoing use of Socratic inquiry. When Socrates wishes to comprehend the uncertain nature of his own death, he turns to an approach based upon questions. Plato thus emphasizes Socrates' indefatigably eager philosophy—one that remains consistently curious even about the nature of its author's demise. In this regard, Socrates' philosophical approach outlasts his own mortal existence.

Perhaps most important, Socrates' words within this section help to accomplish Plato's goal of vindicating his teacher for posterity. Detractors might hold that Socrates could not have been a wise man: had he been, he would have avoided a wrongful execution. Indeed, if Socrates did not discuss his belief in the precedence of virtue over bodily harm, he would in fact appear to be his accusers' victim. However, given the great deliberateness Socrates reveals, we see that he actually does not succumb. In Plato's depiction, Socrates consciously chooses to die, acknowledging his choice not to avoid his sentence so as not to compromise his principles of virtue. By ending the *Apology* in this manner, Plato vindicates Socrates' wrongful death, revealing that the execution in fact comes on Socrates' own virtuous terms.

CRITO, 43A–49A

SUMMARY

Crito begins before dawn in Socrates' prison cell, with the elderly Crito waiting for Socrates to awaken. Crito is unable to stir Socrates, who is calm and tranquil in the face of his imminent execution. Crito admires Socrates' peaceful demeanor and confesses the emotional turmoil he suffers at the prospect of his friend's death. Upon waking, Socrates remarks that a man of his advanced age should hardly despair about death. Crito quickly replies that a man of any age would have reason to despair were they to face a predicament such as Socrates' current one.

Crito notes that the date of Socrates' execution finally has drawn near. Socrates calmly replies that he has had a dream foretelling his death in three days, which prompts Crito to urge Socrates' immediate escape from imprisonment. Crito fears both the loss of his irreplaceable friend and the scorn of society for letting down Socrates in his time of need. Crito knows that no one will recognize Socrates' admirers' attempts to persuade him to flee—but instead will remember only their failure to save Socrates. Crito, unlike Socrates, places importance in popular opinion and worries about its capacity to cause harm. Socrates states his desire that society could be capable of infinite harm, as this condition would entail humanity's simultaneous potential for unlimited good. He regrets, however, that humans have neither ability.

Crito offers that Socrates need not worry about the difficulties of escaping, for his friends and students have already made arrangements on his behalf. Crito assures Socrates that money presents no obstacle, urges him to think of his responsibilities to his children, criticizes his unwillingness to compromise before court and his friends' pleas, and begs him once more to flee.

Socrates expresses gratitude for Crito's sentiments and declares his intention to reflect on his friend's arguments. Such careful consideration of action according to reason has been Socrates' custom throughout his life, and he does not plan to change it simply due to his current situation. He intends to determine the most appropriate course of action via his standard method of inquiry, and subsequently to act according to the dictates of reason. To this end, Socrates begins by proposing that only wise opinions should be considered regarding any matter. He illustrates this point with an analogy to someone in training taking only the advice of experts in his field. Thus, only the judgments of wise advisors, and not those of the public, should be valued when considering any action. Furthermore, just as life is not worth living in a body destroyed by bad health, so too is life meaningless if the part of us in which right and wrong operate is destroyed by bad actions. In fact, this part of our being may possess even greater significance to our existence then our physical selves. As such, it demands this increased level of care.

It follows from these arguments that Socrates and Crito should consider only right and wrong rather than what the masses may think about their actions when evaluating escape. Even though the public may possess the power to put him to death, Socrates remains unaffected by this terminal possibility in considering his course of action. He maintains that only the rightness or wrongness of escape should weigh into his choice. All other concerns, such as his friends' reputations or his family's future, amount to illegitimate public worries—as opposed to valid expert worries. Socrates requests that Crito cease his pleas unless he can convince Socrates of the virtue of escaping. With Crito's assent, the two friends prepare to delve deeper into the matter.

ANALYSIS

This dialogue, consisting of a personal conversation between two longtime friends by candlelight, is the most intimate of the four texts depicting Socrates' trial and death. As such, the *Crito* arguably may be interpreted as the most revealing of these four dialogues as well. Despite its intimacy, the *Crito* nonetheless follows the typical Socratic form of an argument between Socrates and someone else who puts forward an opinion. Socrates claims no knowledge beyond that of his interlocutor, he wishes only to inquire into the true nature of the subjects they discuss, and he is ultimately concerned with exploring virtue and justice—the topics that occupied much of Socrates' attention throughout his lifetime.

Throughout this conversation, Socrates' steady tranquility and willingness to face death at virtue's command are increasingly striking. Socrates patiently relates to Crito that matters of life and death pale in comparison to the issue of right versus wrong. This statement ultimately stems from a conception of the soul's immortality that appears in the *Phaedo*. Socrates' point remains that he should only factor aspects of virtue into his decision about whether or not to escape. To defy such considerations in favor of public opinion or distaste for death would be an unacceptable compromise of the most important factors in any decision—those of justice. As the dialogue progresses, we see clearly how strongly Socrates is committed to these principles. Not only does Socrates state that he prefers dying virtuously to living through a breach of principles, but he also follows through and lives this belief.

With this detailed depiction of the exchange with Crito, Plato crystallizes his portrait of Socrates' philosophy and commitment to virtue even beyond death. As with the *Euthyphro* and *Apology*, Plato's goal in writing the *Crito* is partly to commemorate Socrates' life and philosophy. Plato's account of the conversation between Socrates and Crito conveys the essence of Socrates' philosophy—the ultimate pursuit of virtue in all activities. Furthermore, in showing how firmly Socrates adheres to this ethical ideal, even choosing death over life through dishonorable escape, Plato portrays the fierce strength of Socrates' commitment to his teachings. Consequently, the words contained in the *Crito* paint a fairly detailed portrait of Socrates for the rest of the world to regard.

The *Crito* also serves to vindicate Socrates' death. Some of Socrates' contemporaries might be inclined to fault Socrates for his inability to avoid death at the hands of supposedly lesser men than he. With this account, however, Plato emphasizes that Socrates chooses his own death by deciding not to take advantage of the escape opportunity Crito presents. Moreover, Plato insists that Socrates chooses death in order to uphold the very virtue and piety his prosecutors accuse him of destroying in Athenian society. Plato intends to capture the tragic contradiction and irony of these circumstances for posterity. In this regard, Plato thus both memorializes and justifies his mentor's life and death, defining them in terms of Socrates' relentless pursuit of and commitment to the dictates of virtue.

CRITO, 49A–54E

SUMMARY

*"[I]f any one of you stands his ground when he can see
how we administer justice . . . by doing so he has in fact
undertaken to do anything that we tell him. . . ."*
                    (See QUOTATIONS, *p. 56)*

Socrates and Crito agree that no circumstances render wrongdoing acceptable. Even when one has suffered wrong, it remains unacceptable to commit evil. Socrates acknowledges that most people do not share this opinion, and he urges Crito to consent only when he actually agrees rather than merely in order to humor Socrates. Crito nonetheless maintains his position and continues to agree with Socrates' assertions, noting that one ought to fulfill all agreements into which one has entered. Given the agreement Socrates has made with Athens, therefore, his departure without his government's acceptance represents an injury to his state and as such cannot be condoned.

In order to clarify his position, Socrates personifies the Laws of Athens so that they may defend themselves against the prospect of his premature departure. The personified Laws declare that Socrates would effectively destroy his city by rejecting the edicts that regulate its functioning. Crito accepts this point. Next, Socrates imagines nullifying his agreement with the laws by rejecting their decrees. He has benefited throughout his life from accepting the laws—they have provided a structure for marriage, for the upbringing of children, and for his own education when he was young—so he cannot now justify the decision to reject them. Just as a child should not disobey his parents, Socrates should not suddenly choose to operate outside the law, as the state and its rules are of far greater importance than a single individual. Consequently, if Socrates cannot persuade his country to allow his escape, he must not even attempt to flee. Crito agrees with this conclusion.

Next, the personified Laws declare that Socrates has entered into an understanding with Athens simply by virtue of his choice not to depart the state when he first became an adult and could have done so. Nothing in the laws prevents any citizen from leaving, so an individual's choice not to move elsewhere amounts to a willingness to live according to the laws of the state in which one chooses to live. Any failure to do so signifies a rejection of one's parents and guardians as well as a general civic disobedience.

SUMMARY & ANALYSIS

In this regard, flight would render Socrates one of Athens' most guilty offenders and as such cannot be an acceptable course of action. This is so especially given Socrates' seventy years of willing, rewarding obligation to Athens and its laws. As the Laws describe, any breach of this agreement on Socrates' part constitutes a betrayal of himself and his friends rather than a benefit to himself and them. Furthermore, no foreign state could desire Socrates' presence after such an inappropriate defection, as there would be no evidence of his intent to remain obliged to the foreign set of laws either. By this reasoning, the personified Laws conclude that Socrates would have nowhere else suitable to live should he decide to flee Athens.

The sole option left to Socrates, then, is to follow the Laws' advice and remain in Athens—the only course of behavior that embodies the proper path. To further justify this claim, the Laws mention that only such virtuous action will assist Socrates' situation with the immortal judges of the afterlife. Though Socrates' death is an injustice suffered at the hands of others, if Socrates were to choose to escape in the dishonorable fashion considered in the *Crito*, he would add dishonor to his death. In short, despite the injustice of Socrates' circumstances, flight would essentially constitute a breach of contract.

Due to the injury to himself, his friends, and his family that would result from an unapproved escape, Socrates finds it unacceptable to attempt such an action. He emphatically expresses this view, as well as its origins in the voice that sometimes guides his thoughts. Crito has nothing further to add to this consideration of immediate departure, so Socrates asks his friend to allow him to die without further pleas for flight, and the dialogue ends.

ANALYSIS

The second half of the *Crito* centers on an idea that is essentially an ancient prototype of the social contract. To introduce this idea of the social contract, Plato employs an uncharacteristic narrative technique by personifying the Laws of Athens. This device is unusual within Plato's writing and is a rather enigmatic choice on his part. However, the move is purposeful, as Plato's decision to personify the Laws allows Socrates to engage in a dynamic exchange about the propriety of escape. This exchange permits the philosopher to discourse with the Laws as he would with another individual. In this light, this personification and conversation are consistent with Socrates' style elsewhere. In short, Plato resorts to an unusual narrative technique to preserve the Socratic style of question and answer. The resulting portrayal is of a Socrates so intent upon questioning the acceptability of escape that he personifies inanimate laws in order to engage them in a traditional dialogue about the matter.

Socrates' debate with the personified Laws leads to a discussion of civic obligation, which is one of the earliest treatments of this important concept on record. The basic framework for social duty stems from an adult's voluntary relationship with his or her state. To be sure, no young person possesses sufficient autonomy to decide legitimately between staying in or departing a state based on its customs: children, then, remain in any given society because of their parents, who themselves have chosen their current homeland. A youth's departure without permission represents a defiance of family rather than of the state.

When a person reaches adulthood, however, his or her relationship with the laws changes. At this point, people may freely choose to relocate to more preferable locations should they determine the rules and customs of their homeland to be less desirable than those of other countries. Furthermore, any person who does *not* relocate at the onset of adulthood in order to access more favorable laws effectively enters into a formal, though unspoken, agreement with his or her homeland's laws. This fact arises from the very nature of laws—namely, that they depend upon the people's approval in order to maintain their authority. It is simply contradictory to inhabit a territory willingly while intentionally rejecting that territory's rules.

From this line of reasoning, Socrates concludes that no citizens who have implicitly and voluntarily subscribed to their nation's laws may subsequently choose to reject these laws at their convenience. This course of action displays too deep a disregard for virtue to be acceptable—especially for Socrates, given the seventy years of satisfying life he has sustained under the authority of Athenian law. In light of these seven decades of accord, his flight now would embody especially unjustifiable behavior. Therefore, Socrates emphatically refuses to flee, and thereby creates an early form of social contract.

PHAEDO, 57A–70B

SUMMARY

"[I]t is a fact, Simmias, that true philosophers make dying their profession, and that to them of all men death is least alarming."

(*See* QUOTATIONS, *p. 57*)

Phaedo's reenactment of Socrates' death occurs in the town of Phlius, which plays host to several of Socrates' sympathizers. Only one of these men, Echecrates, actually speaks to Phaedo in the dialogue. Phaedo reveals he was present before and during Socrates' execution, prompting Echecrates to request that Phaedo recount these events to the current audience.

Phaedo begins his story by declaring that he does not feel sorrow for Socrates, for the philosopher maintains a reassuringly serene demeanor in spite of his impending death. Phaedo names those present in the prison cell, specifically noting Plato's absence, presumably owing to sickness. Furthermore, Phaedo alludes to their awareness that day of Socrates' imminent death. Socrates himself knows the moment of his execution has nearly come, and he wonders at the close connection between pain and pleasure. Without further elaboration on this comment, he proclaims his simultaneous willingness to die and refusal to commit suicide—a position that prompts an admirer, Cebes, to question Socrates' meaning. In response, Socrates claims that humans are the possessions of the gods. Just as we would be unhappy should something of ours decide to destroy itself, so too would the gods disapprove of a decision on our part to commit suicide. This impiety renders suicide fundamentally forbidden.

At this point, another man, Simmias, presses Socrates to clarify the basis of his statement that the true philosopher "should be cheerful in the face of death, and confident of finding the greatest blessing in the next world when his life is finished." Socrates replies that he hopes to present himself more successfully here than at his trial, and Simmias assumes the role of interlocutor.

Socrates and Simmias concur that death consists of the separation of body from soul, and nothing more. Furthermore, Socrates holds that good philosophers, while alive, attempt to minimize their bodily concerns in favor of spiritual ones, since the body hinders the soul's attainment of pure virtue and truth. As such, philosophers actually attempt to enact during life the same split between soul and body that occurs in death—though only in death itself may this separation fully occur. Therefore, the wise man welcomes death and its promise for the attainment of true knowledge and goodness. Philosophers therefore claim dying as their profession, while those who despair of dying place their bodies above wisdom. Furthermore, courage and self-discipline belong to the pursuit of philosophy, for they embody the inherent results of wisdom. Socrates himself concedes he has devoted his own life to such pursuits, which justifies his current acceptance of the prospect of death.

Cebes agrees with most of Socrates' claims. However, Cebes feels doubt as to the existence of souls beyond their current bodies' lifetime, as he believes that such a position depends upon an as yet unjustified conception of the afterlife. Cebes does, however, desire an explanation, and he requests that Socrates further elucidate this conception. Socrates willingly accepts Cebes' invitation to talk more.

ANALYSIS

Unlike the other dialogues depicting Socrates' trial and death, *Phaedo* recounts these events indirectly. Our only access to Socrates' death is through a thirdhand view of a secondhand account provided by a firsthand witness of the death. In a sense, the silent audience present for Phaedo's story therefore represent the scores of people who learn of Socrates' death only through Plato's indirect retelling of it. More significant, this narrative distance also highlights the philosophical nature of what Plato relays to us, as it separates his words from the historical authority of a direct account. Phaedo's enumeration of those present at the execution further emphasizes this nonhistorical focus—especially in light of Plato's conspicuous absence, which implies his physical and emotional removal from the events he records. These features all help to convey the specific manipulation within *Phaedo*'s version of Socrates' execution, as they explicitly distance this dialogue from the events it portrays.

Aside from this distanced narrative structure, the *Phaedo* is, in most respects, another quintessentially Socratic dialogue. The Socratic style is evident in Simmias's immediate willingness to take up the role of Socrates' interlocutor. As in other dialogues, we see Socrates and his friends enthusiastically embark upon a quest to discover the true nature of that which they question rather than Socrates simply dictating such knowledge to his friends. Consequently, the method employed in *Phaedo* once again reveals Socrates' standard method of philosophical investigation.

As in the earlier dialogues, Socrates again expresses the basic philosophy pervading his entire life: the ultimate moral ideal of a pure virtuous soul as a guide to all action. Socrates devotes the majority of his career to pursuing and teaching virtue above all other considerations, and his unconcern about death stems directly from his belief in the vast importance of basic goodness. Because the *Phaedo* presents a consideration of death according to Socrates' doctrine of justice, it stands as emblematic of his entire philosophical approach.

At this point, we might object that the merit of focusing exclusively upon matters of the soul requires that we accept Socrates' conception of death and virtue. If we do not agree with him about this, such a focus appears undesirable. This line of reasoning, however, misses a crucial point. The question amounts not to whether we accept Socrates' framework, but whether he himself does: Socrates is attempting only to prove that *pure philosophers* desire their soul's separation from the body—not that *all people* comprehend this situation. Socrates therefore would respond that any person who does not accept his position is not a true philosopher, precisely because that person has not yet perceived the primacy of the spiritual realm and its hindrance by the bodily realm.

This argument again helps Plato to accomplish his goal of vindicating Socrates' death at the hands of his prosecutors. Plato successfully conveys that Socrates welcomes his death, and that, in fact, he has welcomed death for his whole life. Rather than impede Socrates' lifelong quest for the attainment of pure knowledge and virtue, then, his execution accelerates the completion of this quest. From this perspective, Socrates' death is a reward that he knowingly welcomes—an acceptance of his death that vindicates Socrates for posterity.

PHAEDO, 70C–84C

SUMMARY

Socrates renews the discourse by mentioning an ancient legend that our souls exist in another world. Since the living come into being from the dead, the dead must still exist as souls in other realms. Next, Socrates proposes that everything generated in the world comes from its opposite—this is by law, for from opposites come opposites. For example, if something becomes bigger, it must first have been smaller; likewise, for something to become smaller, it must first have been bigger. This relation necessarily holds for all properties of existence, such as stronger versus weaker, higher versus lower, and so on. From this reasoning, it follows that death and life—merely another pair of opposites—must generate each other. From death comes life and vice versa, over and over indefinitely. As a consequence, our souls must exist in another world so that they may continually regenerate life in this one. Coming back to life must therefore take place equally endlessly.

Having successfully delivered this argument about opposites, Socrates goes on to prove his theory of recollection. Essentially, this doctrine maintains that learning amounts to recollecting, requiring our souls' existence before—and thus after—our current lifetime. Socrates asserts that humans possess knowledge of both partial and absolute properties, such as that of equality. Furthermore, people may access absolute equality only through instances of partial equality, such as seeing the equal length of two sticks. Thus, absolute equality is something separate from instances of partial equality, yet it is associated with notions of partial equality. Consequently, we must possess knowledge distinct from what we learn during our lives, as we have an abstract basis for comparing particular instances of general properties. Since this prior knowledge of absolutes allows us to understand our experiences as we do, it must exist before our experiences—before birth. Learning thus amounts to remembering, which requires that our souls somehow existed prior to our bodies. This assertion is supported by our inability to describe how we come to comprehend abstract forms of equality and the like.

Simmias and Cebes concede that Socrates reveals the soul's existence prior to inhabiting a body, but they are not convinced that our souls survive beyond our bodily death. Despite Socrates' conviction that he has already proven this point through the argument from opposites, he gladly addresses his peers' concern. He asserts that some things are inconstant, variable, and visible, while others display constant invisibility and invariability—for example, the partial instances versus absolute aspects of a quality such as beauty. The former are fleeting and mortal, while the latter remain eternal and essentially divine. Given that the body hinders the soul's attainment of timeless truth and virtue, it follows that while the body belongs to the corporeal realm, the soul falls under the immortal classification. If a person devotes his life to detaching his soul from his body, this separation in death easily occurs, and the soul moves unencumbered throughout eternity.

Socrates goes so far as to claim that the mythical underworld figures of Hades are those souls who were not able to slip smoothly away from their bodies, since our current pursuits determine our ability to do so upon dying. Philosophy and the pursuit of truth therefore provide the soul with a route of escape from its bodily confines while alive, in preparation for death's separation, for the body is excluded from connecting to the divine, while the soul is our means to such holy access.

ANALYSIS

Socrates' arguments in this section reveal Plato's gradually emerging independent philosophical voice. Unlike the other three dialogues on Socrates' trial and death, therefore, the *Phaedo* is a later, less Socratic writing—it generally is regarded as the final text of Plato's early period. Consequently, Socrates' arguments from Opposites, Recollection, and Affinity embody Plato's own ideas at least as much as they do those of his teacher.

Plato's distinctive voice emerges most clearly within the argument from Recollection. This formulation of the soul's immortality crucially depends upon Plato's famous Theory of Forms—his timeless account of the ideal existence of all properties. These are the entities to which Socrates refers when he discusses the absolute Forms of qualities such as beauty, justice, and the like in his consideration of experiential versus innate knowledge. Because we possess knowledge of the complete Forms prior to interacting with incomplete physical reality (knowledge that is necessary to comprehend these interactions), some part of us other than our bodies must exist before our birth. Undying souls are the only option. In this sense, the soul's immortality derives directly from the nature of Forms.

Plato's three arguments for immortality unify Socrates' most significant claims up to this point. The arguments in the previous dialogues indicate that Socrates' belief in the importance of virtue results from his conception of death and the afterlife. Each time Socrates maintains the supremacy of virtue, even in the face of death, he depends upon a conception of dying that remains unspecified—until now. These sections reveal exactly why matters of proper action trump any concern for death: because our souls—the parts of humans in which virtue exists—live on past bodily death. To ignore virtue in favor of physical life, therefore, is to ignore the facts about physical death and our spiritual lives beyond it. Socrates' decisions and philosophy center upon the ethical focus of virtue, and he relies upon his belief in existence beyond physical forms to justify this version of morality. Plato, by providing arguments for such a conception of the soul's immortality, thus helps to account for and legitimize Socrates' beliefs.

Plato accomplishes this support mission on Socrates' behalf through his narrative choices. For example, Socrates refers to mythological example as evidence for his actions and his conception of the afterlife. By doing so, he implies that the very religion of Athens attests to his innocence, whereas the court of Athens finds him guilty. Such narrative manipulation helps Plato strengthen Socrates' position as he establishes it throughout this dialogue.

Furthermore, Plato offers what can be seen as Socrates' ultimate vindication—his discussion of philosophy as a means by which to escape the prison of mortality. This statement incorporates Socrates' fundamental philosophy and as such might be taken at face value. Simultaneously, however, this assertion also possesses deeper significance. Though Socrates himself is about to die, he remains utterly serene and even welcomes this approaching fate. Socrates' enemies sentence him to death in order to punish him, as they believe death to be the worst of all evils. Socrates, however, makes clear that, contrary to seeing dying as the supreme evil, he views it as a sure means to attain what he continuously strives for— pure knowledge and virtue unfettered by corporeal confines. By clarifying this philosophy, Plato defends Socrates' death, showing that Socrates has always desired what awaits him.

PHAEDO, 84C–103B

SUMMARY

Simmias voices an objection to Socrates' claims, making an analogy between the strings and tuning of a musical instrument and the human body and soul. Just as tuning imparts an incorporeal, ethereal quality to the physical strings, so too does the human soul to the physical body. According to Socrates' belief in the soul surviving its body's death, a given tuning also would have to survive its instrument's destruction. As this surely cannot be the case, Socrates' story about souls existing beyond their bodies seems inadequate.

Socrates accepts this criticism, but entertains another from Cebes before responding. Cebes' worry is simple: he accepts Socrates' vision of the soul's afterlife but feels it does not follow from the position that the soul must be immortal. Cebes compares the soul's situation to that of a tailor who outlasts several of his own coats though he himself is not immortal. This appears to oppose Socrates' stance. At this point, Phaedo confesses to his audience the despair sensed by those present in the cell at the introduction of such legitimate objections to Socrates' beliefs.

Socrates appears receptive to these well-formed criticisms, and he willingly responds to his challengers. He attributes his openness to debate to an attempt at perfecting his intellect by relentlessly seeking out the validity of all claims. Socrates invites dissent to any of his points so long as it is carefully formed dissent. In response to Simmias's criticism, Socrates states that Simmias must alter his conception of attunement if he accepts the previous theory of Recollection. Under Recollection, the soul cannot resemble composite attunement, for it exists prior to the body, excluding the possibility of the soul arising from composite physical elements. As such, Socrates reveals that Simmias's position rests upon a mistaken analogy between souls and tuning. This fact follows from the primacy of the theory of Recollection and provides evidence for the soul's control over the body.

Socrates then revisits Cebes' claim against his framework of immortality. He acknowledges the legitimacy of Cebes' criticism, saying that it merits a full investigation of the nature of causation—the study of generation and destruction. Socrates also describes his rich experience with the perplexity of these nebulous matters as well as his lack of success at such inquiries. As a means to delve into causation once more, the philosopher refers back to his theory of absolute properties such as beauty, magnitude, and the like. Cebes grants Socrates the existence of such fundamental entities, and Socrates goes on to declare that anything manifesting a property like beauty does so inasmuch as it participates in the ideal Form of this property. This situation pertains to all qualities of existence, and from it Socrates concludes that the Forms exist as the causes of all other things. Anything tall, for example, is tall because it partakes of the Form tallness to a certain degree. Socrates offers several such examples. Opposite absolutes entirely refrain from participating in one another— tallness cannot be short, beauty cannot be ugly. Socrates carefully distinguishes this point about opposites *themselves* from an earlier one regarding opposite *objects and events*—features that he argued emerge from each other.

ANALYSIS

Both Simmias's and Cebes' objections are taken very seriously by Socrates, and answering them occupies much of the rest of the dialogue. Socrates welcomes objections, as he sees them as further fuel for an interesting debate. Here especially, we come to appreciate the literary force of the dialogue form in Plato's writing. Plato does not simply wish to impose his opinions upon us, but rather wants us to think them through and sort them out for ourselves. Only through a dialectic method, complete with counterarguments and objections, can we be brought to consider the matter for ourselves and gain true knowledge of it.

Simmias's objection comparing the soul to the attunement of a musical instrument is closely linked to Pythagorean thought. The Pythagoreans believed in the divinity of music and in the notion that the motion of the celestial spheres is dictated by perfect harmonies. It is natural, then, for a Pythagorean like Simmias to think of the soul as a harmony. This idea brings in a different view of the soul altogether. In Socrates' account, the soul is something distinct from the parts of the human body, something that enters the body and imbues it life, but that can exist independently of it. For Simmias, the soul is not a distinct entity so much as the force by which all the parts of the body are held together and through which all the parts of the body are related. The soul gives the body life, but has no life independent of the body, in this view. Thus, the soul cannot exist without the body.

Cebes' objection borrows more from Heraclitus. The Heraclitean theory that all is in flux suggests that there is no such thing as enduring physical objects. For instance, my body is slightly different from what it was five minutes ago. According to Heraclitus, this means that my body now is a different body from the body I had five minutes ago. Essentially, Heraclitus applies to the whole world the principle that you can never step in the same river twice, suggesting that at every instant the world is destroyed and remade in a slightly different form. According to Cebes' argument, then, the many bodies that a soul may inhabit are not the bodies of different people spread out over centuries, but the many bodies of one person, each one being remade at every instant.

The brief interlude in which Phaedo and Echecrates remark on the weight of Simmias's and Cebes' objections is one of only two breaks in Phaedo's account. This interlude serves to remind us of the complex framing of the narrative and of the fictitiousness of the whole account. Plato frames the story in this way—even making explicit mention of his own absence at Socrates' death—to make it clear that he is not describing the events as they actually took place. Instead, he is using that setting as a powerful backdrop against which he can present some of his own views. In reminding us of this fictitiousness, Plato is also reminding us that we are not reading a story with the intent to find out "what happened," but rather are reading philosophy with the intent to think for ourselves and to tease out the truth.

PHAEDO, 103C–118

SUMMARY

Cebes and Simmias agree that opposites never can oppose themselves. Socrates asserts that snow, though itself distinct from coldness, cannot possess the characteristic of heat and still remain snow. Similarly, odd numbers are distinct from oddness, but nonetheless cannot admit of evenness while persisting as odd. Thus, properties comprising some Forms always pertain to certain other entities—themselves not these Forms but rather identified by them. Socrates concludes that some objects that are always distinguished by, though do not constitute, certain absolute properties, also themselves refuse the absolutes' opposing properties—as do the Forms themselves: "There are other things too which cannot face the approach of opposites." This inability emerges from any automatic incompatibility between an entity manifesting a certain Form and that Form's opposite. In this regard, the Form of evenness may enter neither into the Form of oddness nor the Form of threeness.

Next, Socrates maintains that vitality always accompanies Soul, whenever life occurs in a body. Furthermore, life has an opposite, in death. From the above argument it becomes clear that the soul can never admit of death, since life—which itself automatically refuses death—always comes with the presence of Soul. Since that which does not admit death is immortal, and the soul does not admit death, the soul must be immortal, imperishable, and never can die. For this reason, when someone body dies, his or her immortal soul recedes from the body's lifelessness.

With this final major argument in place, Socrates reiterates the importance of attention to the soul's eternal well-being, especially in light of these most recent considerations. He relays a detailed myth of the afterlife meant to convey the urgency of his message. To this end, he depicts the lost, suffering souls of those who focus excessively on the body while occupying this world. Socrates describes a vast reality of truth and appearances, of which humans inhabit merely a shallow segment. Only the wisest men—true philosophers—obtain immediate access, through divine judgment, to the deeper levels of pure truth and virtue. These true philosophers obtain this access only because of their continued commitment to knowledge and the soul over the body. All others are certain to remain unaware of such realms. In this way, Socrates conclusively describes his fate as that of the sage.

Before ingesting his poison, Socrates leaves his friends with some last words. He advises them to take heed of what he has said and to endeavor to enact his teachings while they live—for they too shall face death. The philosopher then departs for a bath, while the others remain. He calmly bathes, bids farewell to his family, and returns to his cell and admirers. A guard apologetically brings Socrates the infamous hemlock. Socrates expresses his desire not to delay drinking it, as he has long since finished clinging to life. He offers hopes for prosperity in the afterlife, prompting tears from many in attendance. Socrates rebukes his friends, stating that the women have been sent home in order to avoid such sobbing. This remark quiets the crowd. Socrates cheerfully drinks his poison, humbly asks that Crito offer a sacrifice to the god of healing, and calmly slips into the afterlife. In this manner the dialogue closes.

ANALYSIS

This final section of the *Phaedo* reveals some of Plato's more sophisticated and complex philosophical ideas. The formulations here stand in fairly stark contrast to the simpler Socratic ideas presented in earlier dialogues. The main thrust of the *Phaedo* is Plato's utilization of a version of his famous Theory of Forms in order to demonstrate beyond all doubt the soul's immortality. Plato reintroduces the notion of essential properties in Socrates' discussion of heat as essential to fire and oddness to the quantity three. From this relationship Plato draws a parallel to life as an essential quality of the soul, since bodies only—and always—exist when souls occupy them. It follows that souls are immortal.

It is worth noting that this crucial argument, made immediately prior to Socrates' execution, hinges upon a clearly Platonic (and thus post-Socratic) philosophical stance. Some might object that Plato, in using post-Socratic ideas to describe Socrates' death, takes too much creative license here. At the same time, though, this choice on Plato's part represents a profound effort to vindicate Socrates' execution for posterity, for every argument Socrates offers in defense of his willingness to die depends upon death being a separation of the soul from the body. He believes that such a separation implies a duty to focus on his soul's virtue rather than its bodily hindrances, and he believes that as a philosopher he has more than adequately fulfilled this obligation. If Plato can provide sufficient justification for this view of death, then he can show Socrates to triumph by dying—for doing so permits him to achieve ultimate knowledge, virtue, and freedom. It is exactly this type of passing that has been the focus of Socrates' lifelong preparation; therefore, if its basis is correct, he stands to enjoy a rich eternity beyond his execution.

Plato explains the relationship between Forms and objects in the world by saying that things "participate" in the Forms. It is not entirely clear what he means by this, but there are three likely possibilities of what Forms are according to this claim. The first is that Forms are paradigms, the perfect instances of whatever they represent. For instance, the Form of Justice is the paradigm of justice, the one most perfect instance of justice in this world. All other things that are just are just only insofar as they emulate, or are similar to, this Form of Justice. The second explanation is that Forms are universals—that which all instances of the Form have in common. The Form of Justice is that quality which all just people have in common. According to this interpretation, one participates in the Form of Justice by sharing in that quality of justice. The third explanation is that Forms are "stuffs" distributed throughout the world. The Form of Justice, under this interpretation, is not some separate thing but is rather the sum of all the instances of justice that we might find in the world. There is a little bit of justice in me, there is a little bit of justice in you, and if we were to gather all these little bits of justice together, we would have the Form of Justice. Thus, each of us participates in the Form of Justice by having a bit of the Form in us, like sharing a small piece of a very big pie.

IMPORTANT QUOTATIONS EXPLAINED

1. "[T]he holy is loved [by the gods] because it is holy, and not holy because it is loved. . . ."

This statement, from the *Euthyphro* (10e), is the heart of Socrates' argument against Euthyphro's descriptions of piety. Socrates asks Euthyphro to define a general property common to all instances of holiness, and Euthyphro responds that what is pious is that which all the gods love. In other words, anything all the gods love is holy because the gods unanimously love it. Socrates' objection is that such a conception does not suffice. Whatever the gods love, they love it *as a result* of something about the thing they love—namely, its holiness. Given this state of affairs, something cannot be deemed holy because the gods love it, since the gods love it *because* it is holy. Socrates' rebuttal reveals the incoherence of Euthyphro's position.

Socrates' argument here hinges upon a distinction between two different types of aspects any object or being might possess. Accidental properties are features something possesses in virtue of some state in which it happens to find itself. For example, a bag's accidental property of being carried results from its state of being carried rather than the other way around. The bag does not *get* carried because it *is* carried, instead it *is* carried because it *gets* carried. At the same time, essential properties, such as fire's heat, are fundamental aspects of the beings, objects, or entities to which they apply. This distinction foreshadows aspects of Plato's Theory of Forms and causation, which Socrates voices later in the *Phaedo*.

2.   "The wisest of you men is he who has realized, like Socrates,
      that in respect of wisdom he is really worthless."

Socrates offers these words, in the *Apology* (23b), as his interpretation of the Oracle at Delphi's proclamation that he is the wisest of all
men. This statement represents the heart of Socrates' inquisitive
philosophical approach. After hearing that the Oracle extols his
wisdom, Socrates sets out to interview several different types of
experts in various fields with the hopes of learning exactly what
might be his own expertise. Throughout the course of these interviews, Socrates becomes aware of how little these supposed experts
truly seem to know. From this pattern, he concludes that his wisdom
must consist of the perception of just how little all people—including himself—actually comprehend. This lack of understanding
motivates Socrates' insatiable thirst for knowledge and endless
questioning, at least as Plato portrays him. Indeed, Socrates' famous
professions of ignorance comprise both the foundation of his own
particular brand of philosophy and an effective revolution from previous methods of understanding. Unfortunately for Socrates, his
preaching of human ignorance also earns him the animosity of those
who eventually execute him.

3. "You are mistaken, my friend, if you think that a man who is worth anything ought to spend his time weighing up the prospects of life and death. He has only one thing to consider in performing any action—that is, whether he is acting rightly or wrongly, like a good man or a bad one."

In these words, from the *Apology* (28b), Socrates voices what is arguably his fundamental ethical belief—that considerations of virtue are the only important factors in any decision. In this context, however, Socrates offers this idea to justify his lack of concern about death. In essence, Socrates feels that no true harm can befall him so long as his actions exhibit virtue. Though his prosecutors may convict him and put him to death, proper choices on his part protect him from a greater evil—that of the soul. For this reason, Socrates declares himself unable to cease his teachings in spite of their civil consequences, since to do so would be to defy the gods for mortal, bodily considerations—a truly unjustifiable act. This refusal to halt in turn causes the jury to choose execution as Socrates' fate. In a sense, then, Socrates' commitment to virtue as expressed in this quotation eventually leads to his death.

QUOTATIONS

4. "[I]f any one of you stands his ground when he can see how we administer justice and the rest of our public organization, we hold that by doing so he has in fact undertaken to do anything that we tell him. . . ."

These ideas, spoken by Socrates' personification of the Laws of Athens in the *Crito* (51e), are intended as a reply to Crito's efforts to persuade Socrates to escape. As Socrates' execution draws near, Crito wishes Socrates to consider not only his own well-being, but also that of his students, friends, and family. Socrates, however, maintains that not only would an escape express a lack of virtue, but it would also counteract prior decisions he has made. Specifically, for seventy years Socrates has lived in Athens happily, fully accepting the ways and laws of his city. Since he has been tried, convicted, and sentenced by these very same laws—the ones he here attempts to personify—to flee from their verdict would be to lack sense, courage, and virtue. As such, this passage may be construed as an early form of social contract between people and their laws. Because Socrates vocalizes the reasoning of an ideal democratic citizen, it is ironic that he is soon to die in the hands of a government famous for founding the very concept of democracy.

5. "[I]t is a fact, Simmias, that true philosophers make dying their profession, and that to them of all men death is least alarming."

Socrates justifies his lack of concern for death with this statement in the *Phaedo* (68a). As he describes to his admirers in his prison cell, he believes the body corrupts true wisdom and virtue. From this view, it follows that true pursuers of wisdom—philosophers— should desire their soul's separation from the frivolous needs and temptations that automatically result from the soul's combination with the human body. Ever the philosopher, Socrates welcomes death and the benefits it promises in his relentless search for pure knowledge. With this assertion, we see that rather than fear death, Socrates has made the freedom of dying his life's goal.

KEY FACTS

FULL TITLE
> *The Trial and Death of Socrates: Four Dialogues: Euthyphro, Apology, Crito, Phaedo*

AUTHOR
> Plato

TYPE OF WORK
> Philosophical treatise; dialogue (though the *Apology* includes both monologue and dialogue)

LANGUAGE
> Ancient (Classical or Attic) Greek

TIME AND PLACE WRITTEN
> Early fourth century b.c., Athens

DATE OF FIRST PUBLICATION
> Date of primary publication remains unclear, given the works' age and their existence through informal circulation for some time before formal publication

PUBLISHER
> The most universally recognized publisher of Plato is Henri Estenne (Stephanus), whose 1578 edition of Plato's works provides a standard reference point for future editions. Numbers in the margins of most versions of Plato's writings refer to the Stephanus pages.

MAIN SPEAKER
> Socrates, with Euthyphro, Meletus, Crito, Phaedo, Cebes, and Simmias as other participants

POINT OF VIEW
> Third-person witness to the conversations (except *Phaedo*, which is told in third-person witness to Phaedo's recounting of the conversations surrounding Socrates' death)

TONE
> Socrates tends to remain calm, patient, and inquisitive, while his questioners sometimes become arrogant, impatient, or confused.

His students and friends, however, maintain great reverence for him throughout.

TENSE

Present

SETTING (TIME)

The time immediately surrounding Socrates' trial in 399 B.C.

SETTING (PLACE)

Athens

MAJOR CONFLICT

Socrates disputes the nature of life, death, truth, and the like with various interlocutors, as well as in his own defense.

MAJOR TOPICS

Piety; holiness; law; virtue; truth; death

FORESHADOWING

Socrates alludes to the afterlife as well as to future generations' disapproval of his trial and execution.

KEY FACTS

STUDY QUESTIONS & ESSAY TOPICS

STUDY QUESTIONS

1. *Why might Plato have chosen not to provide a conclusive definition of piety in* EUTHYPHRO?

To answer this question we must consider the first major charge against Socrates—that of heretical impiety. Given that Plato partly intends these four dialogues as a means to vindicate Socrates, the lack of definite resolution in *Euthyphro* begins to make sense. In other words, this first dialogue represents a detailed attempt to reach a rigorous definition of the nature of holiness. Yet the participants fail entirely, emphasizing the elusive nature of the definition they seek. By withholding from the dialogue any clear resolution to this investigation of piousness, Plato calls added attention to Socrates' potential innocence of the charges of impiety he faces: Socrates cannot truly be guilty of impiety if no adequate definition of the concept exists. The point of *Euthyphro* might therefore amount to demonstrating that such a definition is nonexistent or unattainable.

2.   *What is the basis of Socrates' wisdom?*

As Socrates endeavors to make clear in the *Apology,* he believes that
his wisdom consists of an awareness of the general human lack of
knowledge. At some prior point, the Oracle at Delphi prophesied
that Socrates is the wisest of all men. Not previously having enter-
tained this notion, and eager to understand it, Socrates sets out to
discover the scope of his apparently vast wisdom. To this end, he
converses with many supposed experts, including politicians, poets,
and craftsmen. Throughout these discussions, Socrates grows
increasingly aware of these interlocutors' lack of knowledge,
despite their apparent expertise. After seeing this result consistently,
Socrates finally concludes that his special wisdom must consist in a
comprehension of general human ignorance.

3. *According to Socrates, why should the wise man welcome death without fear? Does this mean true philosophers commit suicide the moment they achieve enlightenment?*

According to Socrates, wise men should welcome death because of immortality and the soul's afterlife. As Socrates argues in the *Phaedo*, death fundamentally encompasses a separation of one's soul from one's body. The four arguments for immortality, however, reveal that a soul goes on to survive indefinitely beyond the death of any particular body it might inhabit. True philosophers, perceiving this state of affairs, endeavor while alive to focus entirely on the soul, as they recognize the permanence of the soul versus the fleeting nature of the mortal body. Moreover, one's body only may hinder this attention to the soul through its distractions of temptation, physical requirements such as nourishment, and fallible faculties of perception. From these considerations, it follows that the truly wise should embrace death willingly as a means to free themselves from the confines of any particular body or lifetime.

At the same time, however, this situation does not dictate that all true sages should kill themselves the moment they achieve an understanding of the merit of death. As Socrates makes clear, humans are the possessions of the gods—just as livestock are the possessions of humans. Just as we would not be pleased were one of our livestock to decide to take its own life (thereby destroying that which is ours), so too would the gods disapprove of any human who chooses to commit suicide (thus destroying that which is the gods'). For these reasons, one should welcome—but not cause—one's own death.

QUESTIONS & ESSAYS

Suggested Essay Topics

1. *Which of Euthyphro's definitions of piety do you find most convincing? Consider Socrates' responses when forming your answer.*

2. *What is the difference between the assertions "that which the gods love is holy" and "the gods love that which is holy"?*

3. *In the* APOLOGY, *Socrates argues that there are more important considerations than physical harm, even in the face of death. What exactly does he have in mind? Consider Socrates' conceptions of immortality and the afterlife.*

4. *Assess Socrates' prediction that "if [Athens] put[s] me to death, you will harm yourselves more than me" (*APOLOGY, *30c). What exactly does Socrates mean? Do you agree with his statement? Why or why not?*

5. *What does Plato achieve by personifying the Laws of Athens?*

6. *Are you convinced by Socrates' account of the agreement between citizens and their country's laws? Why or why not? Can you think of any situations in which someone might not have a choice about whether to remain in or to depart a certain country or state?*

7. *Which of Socrates' arguments for the immortality of the soul do you find most successful, and why?*

8. *Do you see any parallels between the deaths of Socrates and Jesus? Explain.*

REVIEW & RESOURCES

QUIZ

1. Which of the following people is *not* mentioned in *Euthyphro*?

   A. Plato
   B. Socrates
   C. Euthyphro
   D. Meletus

2. With which of the following crimes is Socrates charged?

   A. Insubordination
   B. Tax evasion
   C. Corruption of youth
   D. Adultery

3. Why does Socrates reject Euthyphro's definition of piety as "prosecution of wrongdoers"?

   A. Euthyphro neglects to distinguish between more serious and less serious crimes
   B. Punishing criminals amounts to correcting one evil with another
   C. No mortal possesses the ability legitimately to judge other persons
   D. Other acts may also be pious

4. Why does a basic definition of holiness prove so difficult to formulate?

   A. Only the gods truly are capable of holiness
   B. The gods themselves disagree about what is holy
   C. Humans are a fallen species
   D. The ancient Greeks were not religious

5. Which of the following is *not* one of the definitions of piety Euthyphro proposes?

    A.   Pleasing the gods

    B.   Prosecution of criminals

    C.   Care for one's fellow countrymen

    D.   That of which the gods approve

6. How does *Euthyphro* end?

    A.   Socrates takes Euthyphro to court on charges of impiety

    B.   Euthyphro provides a definition of holiness that satisfies Socrates

    C.   Euthyphro departs without having formulated an adequate definition of holiness

    D.   Socrates is convicted in court for charges of impiety

7. For what does Socrates excuse himself early in the *Apology*?

    A.   The impious crimes for which he has been charged

    B.   Any of his past teachings that may have offended his countrymen

    C.   His sometimes annoying method of inquiry

    D.   His ignorance of judicial proceedings

8. To whom does Socrates allude as a reference for his wisdom?

    A.   Meletus

    B.   The Oracle at Delphi

    C.   Crito

    D.   Plato

9. What is Socrates' particular, quintessentially human wisdom?

    A.   His awareness of how little he truly knows

    B.   His understanding of the meaning of virtue

    C.   His ability to resist the temptation of his senses

    D.   His comprehension of human nature

10. Which of the following is *not* a charge against which Socrates defends himself?

   A. Impiety
   B. Espionage
   C. Invention of false gods
   D. Corruption of youth

11. What penalty does Socrates propose for himself upon hearing of his conviction?

   A. A life supported by the state
   B. Exile
   C. Death
   D. A severe fine

12. What is one reason for Socrates' disregard for death?

   A. He has lived a life without sin
   B. He does not wish to grovel in front of the court
   C. His knowledge of the afterlife
   D. He believes considerations of virtue outweigh those of life and death

13. In *Crito*, where does the conversation between Socrates and Crito occur?

   A. Socrates' home
   B. Crito's home
   C. Socrates' cell
   D. The Court of Athens

14. Which of the following is *not* a reason Crito employs in his attempts to convince Socrates to escape?

   A. The shame that Socrates' death will cast upon his friends
   B. Socrates' duty to continue teaching
   C. The fate of Socrates' children
   D. Socrates' potential enjoyment of a life in exile

15. What, according to Socrates, is to be valued above all else?

    A. Piety
    B. A good life
    C. Wealth
    D. Happiness

16. What does Socrates personify in his consideration of whether or not it would be just to escape?

    A. Justice
    B. Virtue
    C. The porch of King Archon
    D. The Laws of Athens

17. Socrates believes that to break even one law would be to:

    A. Reject the entire body of laws
    B. Commit unacceptable treason
    C. Diverge from the virtuous path on which he has traveled for seventy years
    D. All of the above

18. Socrates' conception of the relationship between citizens and their laws amounts to a sort of:

    A. Social hierarchy
    B. Social personification
    C. Social contract
    D. Social marketplace

19. Which of the following is *not* a topic of the *Phaedo*?

    A. Immortality
    B. Epistemology
    C. The nature of souls
    D. The afterlife

20. In *Phaedo*, which of the following people is *not* present for Socrates' death?

    A. Simmias
    B. Cebes
    C. Plato
    D. Socrates

21. Socrates argues for the immortality of souls from:

    A. Recollection
    B. Affinity
    C. Forms
    D. All of the above

22. Which of the following best characterizes Socrates' attitude toward death?

    A. Welcoming
    B. Ignorant
    C. Fearful
    D. Ambivalent

23. Which of the following, according to Socrates, is an essential property of souls?

    A. Bodies
    B. Freedom
    C. Life
    D. Virtue

24. What does Socrates relate to his admirers before he dies?

    A. A myth of the afterlife
    B. A parable of justice
    C. A message for his family
    D. A philosophical riddle

REVIEW & RESOURCES

25. Which of the following best describes Socrates throughout
    Euthyphro, Apology, Crito, and *Phaedo?*

    A. Indignant
    B. Emotional
    C. Intellectual
    D. Inquisitive

Suggestions for Further Reading

NAVIA, LUIS E. *Socrates: The Man and His Philosophy.* Lanham, Maryland: University Press of America, 1985.

PLATO. *Early Socratic Dialogues.* New York: Penguin Classics, 1987.

———. *Gorgias.* Ed. Walter Hamilton. New York: Penguin Classics, 1990.

———. *The Republic.* Ed. Desmond Lee. New York: Penguin Classics, 1990.

———. *The Symposium.* Ed. Christopher Gill. New York: Penguin Classics, 1999.

TAYLOR, C. C. W., R. M. HARE, and JONATHAN BARNES. *Greek Philosophers: Socrates, Plato, and Aristotle.* New York: Oxford University Press, 2001.

XENOPHON. *Conversations of Socrates.* Ed. Robin Waterfield. New York: Penguin Classics, 1990.